中文联盟 ChinesePlus

HSK 标准会话教程 1

HSK Standard Conversational Course 1

HSK BIAOZHUN HUIHUA JIAOCHENG 1

中文联盟平台教学中心　语文出版社教材研究中心　编写

Co-edited by Chinese Plus Platform Teaching and Learning Center and Textbook Research Center of Language & Culture Press

张　会　主编

Lead Author Zhang Hui

语文出版社

·北京·

汉考国际认证
适用于汉语水平考试（HSK）

总策划：谷新矿　静　炜
策　划：邵亦鹏　李佩泽　郑　浩　朱春玲

项目负责人：王锦红
项目组成员：许雪松　姜天琦　孙博雅
黄　蕾　王　轩　高　鹤　李艳娇

主　　编：张　会
英文翻译：Raluca Georgescu（张　露）

图书在版编目（C I P）数据

HSK标准会话教程. 1 / 中文联盟平台教学中心，语文出版社教材研究中心编写 ; 张会主编. -- 北京 : 语文出版社，2021.8（2023.9重印）
ISBN 978-7-5187-1208-3

Ⅰ. ①H… Ⅱ. ①中… ②语… ③张… Ⅲ. ①汉语－口语－对外汉语教学－水平考试－教材 Ⅳ. ①H195.4

中国版本图书馆CIP数据核字（2020）第268531号

责任编辑　许雪松
装帧设计　徐晓森
出　　版　语文出版社
地　　址　北京市东城区朝阳门内南小街51号　100010
电子信箱　ywcbsywp@163.com
排　　版　北京光大印艺文化发展有限公司
印刷装订　北京市科星印刷有限责任公司
发　　行　语文出版社　新华书店经销
规　　格　890mm × 1240mm
开　　本　1 / 16
印　　张　7.75
字　　数　134千字
版　　次　2021年8月第1版
印　　次　2023年9月第2次印刷
定　　价　76.00元

010-65592964（咨询）010-65240052（购书）010-65250075（印装质量）

前言

本系列教材《HSK标准会话教程》共5册，根据汉语水平考试（HSK）大纲一级至四级和汉语水平口语考试（HSKK）大纲初级和中级设计，1–3册分别对应HSK一级、二级、三级大纲，4–5册对应HSK四级大纲。各册教材以《普通话1000句》为蓝本，合理吸收其话题与典型句式，以“考教结合”为目标，“以考促教”“以考促学”，学习者学完每一册后可以获得相应的口语交际能力，参加相应级别汉语水平考试（HSK）。

在编写理念上，这套会话教材吸收了国际中文教学研究成果，遵循教学规律，强调典型语境的示范作用，培养学习者对所学词语的多场景重新组合能力。同时，结合时代发展和教学法革新的需求，借鉴移动学习、在线学习的教学理念，研发了配套动漫和微课,使静态的图书与动态的视频有机结合起来,让学习的过程更加有趣，途径更加宽广，手段更加多样，学习的效果更加显著。教师可以拥有丰富的教学内容和灵活的教学手段，学习者可以拥有活泼的学习气氛和多样的学习形式。

本系列教材的特色：

第一，用框架突出句子结构。在“热身”部分采用独特的图形框架展示句子的结构特点及句型的变换关系，让句子结构一目了然，对培养学习者语言输出过程中的组句能力和语言听读过程中的断句能力非常有帮助。

第二，文化理解促进语言学习。每一课的文化点都是与课文内容相关的文化常识或现当代中国国情，有助于学习者了解语言中蕴含的文化因素和中国的现状，加深对中国语言文化的深层次理解，进而促进语言的学习。

第三，对话与陈述并重。每一课在对话体课文外都提供一个第三人称角度的陈述性段落，不同级别对段落的长短、词语的难度要求不同，目的是从入门阶段就开始培养学习者的语段表达能力，即使是在一级阶段词汇数量不多的情况下，也要让所学的每一个词都能得到充分的运用。

第四，侧重听说技能。课文方面，在词汇大纲范围内，尽量通过日常生活常见的情景，展现中文对话中常用的词语和句子。练习题模拟汉语水平考试题型，围绕听说技能的发展进行训练，具有很强的实用性。

第五，配套资源丰富多样。对话、生词及课后听力练习全部配有音频，方便学习者预习、跟读及教师教学，注重培养学习者在不同情景中得体恰当地运用中文进行交际的能力。第一册和第二册配套“动画课文”，将静态、无声的课文变成有声有色的动画故事，增强了教材的趣味性、可读性，帮助学习者理解对话的含义。第三册至第五册配套短视频微课，为教师教授语法和重点词语或进行翻转课堂教学提供条件，也利于学习者课下预习或复习。具体内容可参阅“中文联盟平台”专题网页（http://hskc.chineseplus.net）。

本套教材在研发过程中得到了语文出版社、五洲网络和汉考国际的大力支持和指导，收到了来自五大洲上百所孔子学院（课堂）中外方院长、教师及中国高校中文教师的意见反馈，集中了众多关心中文教材编纂人士的智慧。我们谨代表编写组对大家表示最衷心的感谢。尽管我们竭尽所能，但仍不免存在这样那样的不足，恳请广大师生和读者朋友在使用过程中随时向我们反馈意见，以便将来进一步完善，使这套教材能够成为广大中文学习者的好帮手。

编写组
2021 年 7 月

Preface

This ***HSK Standard Conversational Course*** series consists of five volumes, designed in accordance with *HSK Test Syllabus* (HSK Levels I-IV) and *Chinese Proficiency Test Syllabus Speaking* (HSKK Primary and Intermediate Levels). Volumes 1 to 3 correspond to the HSK Levels I to III syllabi, and volumes 4 and 5 correspond to the HSK Level IV syllabus. The content for each level is based on *1000 Mandarin Chinese Sentences*, from which various topics and marker sentences are assimilated in a way that fits the intended purposes, namely to "combine testing with teaching" "promote teaching through testing", and "promote learning through testing". Upon completion of each volume, learners will have the necessary communication skills and will be able to attend the corresponding HSK test.

The writing concepts behind this conversational Chinese textbook series draw on research results in the field of teaching Chinese as a foreign language, adhere to teaching rules, and lay stress on the illustrative role typical contexts play, in order to cultivate learners' ability to make full use of the words and expressions they've learned by adapting them to various new contexts. Moreover, changing trends of the times and the need for innovation in pedagogy are considered carefully, thus the following notions are applied: use teaching and learning concepts of mobile learning and online learning for reference, develop animations and micro-lectures to complement the textbooks, and integrate the static with the dynamic by using both textbooks and videos, all these with the purpose of having a more engaging learning process, more extensive channels, and more varied methods, which will ultimately lead to remarkable learning results. Teachers will benefit from the rich teaching content and the flexible teaching methods, while students will enjoy a lively learning atmosphere and varied forms of learning.

The five features of this series are:

First, use of boxes to emphasize sentence structures. In the "Warm-up" section, each sentence is enclosed in distinctive drawn boxes which indicate the sentence structure characteristics and show how sentences may convert from one individual word to a larger chunk, thus making sentence structures become clear at a glance. This system greatly helps cultivate learners' ability to form sentences during the process of language output as well as their ability to break down sentences during the process of listening and reading.

Second, comprehension of cultural aspects boosts the language learning process. The cultural aspects presented in each lesson are in close connection with the content of the texts, being either pieces of general cultural knowledge about China or knowledge specifically regarding modern and contemporary China. These will greatly help cultivate learners' understanding of the cultural elements hidden beneath the language layer and the present situation in China and give them a deeper insight into Chinese language and culture, thus acting as catalysts for the language learning process.

Third, equal importance is attached to both dialogues and narration. Each lesson contains a narrative paragraph presented in the third person to complement the active dialogues. The length of the paragraphs and the difficulty level of the words used differ depending on different levels. The purpose is to cultivate learners' discourse ability right from the threshold level and allow them to make full use of every word they've learned even when they're at Level I with a limited vocabulary.

Fourth, lay stress on speaking and listening skills. By staying within the limits of the HSK vocabulary, the texts employ numerous common scenarios from everyday life to display words and sentences frequently used in Chinese conversation. The drills simulate actual HSK question types, by focusing on training listening and speaking skills in a very practical way.

Fifth, a wide variety of auxiliary resources is offered all throughout the series. All the dialogues, new words and listening drills come with audio recordings, which are very handy for both students to prepare the lessons before class or read along and for teachers to conduct their lessons. These lay emphasis on cultivating learners' ability to communicate in Chinese appropriately and effectively in various contexts. Volume 1 and 2 come with "anime texts", which transform the static, soundless texts into stories full of sound and color, making the books more engaging and more readable, thus helping learners grasp the meaning of the dialogues. Volume 3 to 5 come with short videos of micro-lectures, which are a good resource for teachers to present grammar and key words and expressions or to adopt a flipped classroom system for teaching, as well as for learners to prepare or review lessons. For more details, see the special page under Chinese Plus Platform: http://hskc.chineseplus.net.

During its research and development, this series has received strong support and guidance from Language & Culture Press, Continental Network and Chinese Testing International (CTI). Moreover, generous feedback was presented by Chinese and local directors and teachers from more than one hundred Confucius Institutes (classes) from all five continents as well as from college and university teachers in China, making this the product of a multitude of people who show true interest in textbook compiling. We therefore want to extend our most sincere gratitude on behalf of the compiling team to all those mentioned above. Although we put in all efforts and strived for the best, it is unavoidable that insufficiencies and inadequacies still exist, hence we would like to make a cordial request towards all teachers, students and readers who will use these books to present us their feedback at any time, so that we may continue to perfect them and make these books the best helper for learners of Chinese.

The Authors Team

July, 2021

本册编写说明

本册教材为《HSK 标准会话教程》系列教材的第一册，是中文学习的入门教程，适合零起点在校学生及对中文感兴趣的社会人士等中文学习者使用。

本书词句难度等级依据汉语水平考试大纲一级（HSK 一级），用有限的词语和相对简单的语法规则生成尽可能多的交际句子，语句内容符合学习者的生活实际和认知水平。

另外，为了体现中文词汇的复合特点、充分利用 HSK 大纲词汇，本书对大纲的词语进行了重组。例如，大纲含“中国”和“菜”，本书将其合并成为“中国菜”；大纲含“米饭”和“吃”，本书将其组合成为“吃饭”。

全书共 12 课，每一课建议授课时间为 2–3 课时，全书可以在 30–36 课时内完成。各课以赴华留学生学习和生活的亲身经历为主线串联起来，从两个留学生相识开始，一步一步展开他们在中国的学习和生活轨迹。

每一课都包含热身、课文、生词、语法点、练习和文化点六个部分。

热身部分采用独特的框架结构，将本课重点句式通过结构分解进行展示，用不同颜色、不同形状的图形显示不同位置上词语的功能，让句子的主体结构一目了然；用不同颜色、不同线型的线条连接成不同的句子，相同颜色的线条可以连成一个句子。同时对框内词语进行翻译，既能预习生词，还可以进行中英文句型的对照，使学习者了解中文短语的复合方法和句子的构成规则，从而培养典型语句的结构意识。

课文部分充分反映了会话教材的特点，包括两篇情景对话和一篇叙述性短文，将语言交际能力和个人陈述能力有机结合。两篇对话围绕本课重点语法和句型展开，旨在培养学习者在不同情境下运用同一个语法点进行口语交际的能力；一篇短文与对话内容相关，陈述事实，回顾一天发生的事情，相当于回答“今天做了什么”，目的是训练学习者的话语陈述能力和连贯表达能力。

生词部分按照惯例编排，列出了本课新出现的词语，提供了汉语拼音、词性说明和英文释义。

语法点部分用中英双语解释课文中出现的重点语法和词语，并给出仅用本级词语的典型例句，全书覆盖了 HSK 一级语法大纲的范围。

练习部分参考 HSK 一级和 HSKK 初级考试题型，对本课重点内容进行听说训练，有利于学习者熟悉考试题型，为顺利通过相应级别考试奠定基础。

文化点部分用中英双语介绍一项与本课内容相关的中国语言文化常识或当代中国国情，激发学习者兴趣，扩展其知识面，帮助其积累文化知识、理解中国语言文化。为减轻教材体量，这部分内容将作为网络资源提供给学习者。

本书语句紧扣 HSK 和 HSKK 大纲，内容清新，与时俱进，特色鲜明。初学者可以通过此书快速入门，体会中文学习的乐趣。千里之行，始于足下，让我们一起踏上中文学习之路吧！

编者

2021 年 7 月

A Guide to the Use of This Book

This volume is the first one in the *HSK Standard Conversational Course* series. It is an introductory course for learning Chinese, suitable for school students and other members of the broader community who are just beginning to learn Chinese.

The difficulty level of the words and sentences in this book is based on *HSK Test Syllabus* (HSK Level I). A limited number of words and expressions and fairly simple grammar rules have been used to generate a maximum amount of sentences true to life and tallying with learners' cognitive level.

Moreover, this volume has made full use of the HSK Vocabulary Outline by regrouping the words, in order to exhibit the compounding nature of Chinese words. For instance, the Outline contains the words "China" and "food" and the words "(cooked) rice" and "to eat", so in this book they are combined into "Chinese food" and "to eat (cooked) rice" respectively.

The book contains 12 lessons in total. We suggest each lesson be taught for 2-3 hours, which brings the total amount of time for completing the whole book to 30-36 hours. The lessons are interconnected by a main storyline revolving around the personal experiences of international students living and studying in China. Starting with two international students who become acquainted with each other, step by step the lessons take us onto their path of living and studying in China.

Each lesson comprises six sections, namely Warm-up, Texts, New Words, Language Points, Drills, and Cultural Aspects.

The Warm-up section utilizes a distinctive technique using boxes to break down key sentence structures and different colors and shapes to show how the function of words varies according to their position in the sentence, thus making the primary structure of a sentence become clear at a glance. Different colors and types of lines are used to connect different sentences, and lines with the same color can be connected to form a sentence. Moreover, the words in the boxes are translated so that learners may both prepare the new words in advance and compare Chinese sentence types with English ones, which helps them grasp the rules of compounding phrases and forming sentences in Chinese and become aware of typical sentence structures.

The Texts section fully reflects the qualities of a conversational textbook. It consists of two situational dialogues and one narrative paragraph, which integrate discourse ability with individual narration ability. The two dialogues revolve around key grammar points and sentences from the lesson, intended to help nurture learners' ability to communicate using the same grammar points under various contexts. The narrative paragraph is closely connected to the dialogues, mainly focusing on narrating facts, looking back at the day's events, basically answering the question "What did you do today?", with the purpose of training learners' ability of narrative discourse and coherent expression.

The New Words section lists the new words in each lesson along with their corresponding Pinyin, part of speech and English explanation.

The Language Points section uses both Chinese and English to explain the key grammar points and words and expressions which appear throughout the texts. These are complemented by typical illustrative sentences using words strictly corresponding to this level and covering the HSK Level I grammar outline.

The Drills section is based on HSK Level I and HSKK Primary Level question types. The purpose is to practice listening and speaking based on the main content of the lesson as well as to familiarize learners with actual HSK question types, so that they may have a basis for smoothly going through the test corresponding to their level.

The Cultural Aspects section introduces pieces of general knowledge regarding Chinese language and culture or the present situation in China, all in close connection with the content of the texts. This integration of language with culture captures learners' interests by expanding their scope of knowledge and helps them understand Chinese language and culture by accumulating cultural knowledge. This section will be put online in order to reduce the size of the printed textbook.

The words and sentences in this book are directly connected with the HSK and HSKK syllabi and are presented in a clear and distinctive content with up-to-date information. These features make this book a good option for beginners to easily enter the world of learning Chinese and experience the joy that comes with it. A journey of a thousand miles begins with a single step, let us embark on the journey towards learning Chinese together!

The Author

July, 2021

目录 Contents

语法点
Language Points

1. “叫”：To be called a name/one's name is
2. 疑问代词“什么”：The interrogative pronoun “什么”
3. “是”字句：Sentences with “是”(to be)
4. “你呢”：How about you?/And you?
5. 结构助词“的”：The structural particle “的”

1. 名词谓语句：Noun-predicate sentences
2. 语气助词“了”：The modal particle “了”
3. “几岁”和“多大”：“几岁”and “多大”
4. “零”：Zero
5. 形容词谓语句：Adjective-predicate sentences

1. “怎么”＋动词：“怎么”+verb
2. 能愿动词“会”：The modal verb “会”
3. 主谓谓语句：Subject-predicate predicate sentences
4. “这么”＋动词：“这么”+verb

1. 连动句：Sentences with serial verb phrases
2. 时间名词的位置：Position of time nouns
3. 能愿动词“想”：The modal verb “想”

1. “多少钱”：How much does it cost
2. 表动作完成的“了”：The construction “verb+了+object” to express a completed action
3. 表“拥有”的“有”：“有” The verb to express possession
4. 疑问代词“哪儿”：The interrogative pronoun “哪儿”
5. 钱数的表达：Expressing an amount of money

语法点
Language Points

1. 动词“在”：The verb “在”
2. “那儿”：“那儿” indicates a location
3. 表存在的“有”：“有” expresses the existence
4. “怎么了”：“怎么了” is often used to express a question
5. “一个……一个”：“一个……一个” construction used in enumerating things
6. 方位词“上”“里”：The nouns of locality “上” “里”

1. 能愿动词“能”：The modal verb “能”
2. 心理动词“想”：The psychological verb “想”
3. 介词“在”：The preposition “在”
4. 量词“个”：The measure word “个”
5. 时量补语：Time complements

1. 疑问代词“哪”：The interrogative pronoun “哪”
2. 量词“号”：The measure word “号”
3. 时间的表达方式：Ways of expressing time
4. 语气助词“呢”：The modal particle “呢”
5. 日期的表达方式：Ways of expressing dates

1. 量词“号”：The measure word “号”, which indicates the order
2. 方位词“前面”：The noun of locality “前面”
3. “你怎么了”：“你怎么了” used for inquiry
4. 副词“多”：The adverb “多”, which modifies the verb

1. 疑问代词“怎么样”：The interrogative pronoun “怎么样”
2. 副词“都”：The adverb “都”
3. “太……了”：The construction “太……了” forms an exclamatory sentence
4. “不客气”：Polite expression “不客气”
5. “好”+感官动词：The construction “好”+sensory verb is used to express a type of positive sensation

语法点
Language Points

1. “呢”：“呢” Used together with “在” to form the construction “在……呢”
2. “在”＋动词＋（宾语）＋“呢”：“在”+verb+(object)+“呢” expresses an action in progress at the moment of speech
3. 动词＋“了”＋（数量词）宾语：verb +“了”+ (quantifier) object

1. “是……的”：“是……的” A type of sentence construction used for emphasis
2. “不……不……”：“不……不……” Used in front of words or morphemes belonging to the same category but with opposite meanings
3. “认识你很高兴”：“认识你很高兴” Common expression used when meeting someone for the first time
4. “这几天”：“这几天” indicates the few recent days
5. “一家人”：“一家人” indicates the whole family

书中主人公是两名在中国学习中文的留学生。书中内容以其在中国生活与学习的亲身经历为主线。

The main characters in the book are two international students studying Chinese in China. The stories in the book revolve around their personal experiences living and studying in China.

大卫，男，英国人，预科生，准备在中国一所大学读中国历史。

David, male, British, preparatory course student, preparing to study a major in Chinese History at a university in China.

莎莉，女，来自墨西哥，大卫的同学。

Sally, female, from Mexico, David's classmate.

另外，本书还有两个人经常出现在主人公的生活中。他们是：

In addition, there are two more people who often appear in the main characters' lives. They are:

尼克，男，美国人，在中国工作五年了，大卫的朋友。

Nick, male, American, working for five years in China, David's friend.

王华，女，大卫的中文老师。

Wang Hua, female, David's Chinese language teacher.

1 Lesson One

Wǒ shì nǐmen de Zhōngwén lǎoshī

我是你们的中文老师

I am your Chinese language teacher

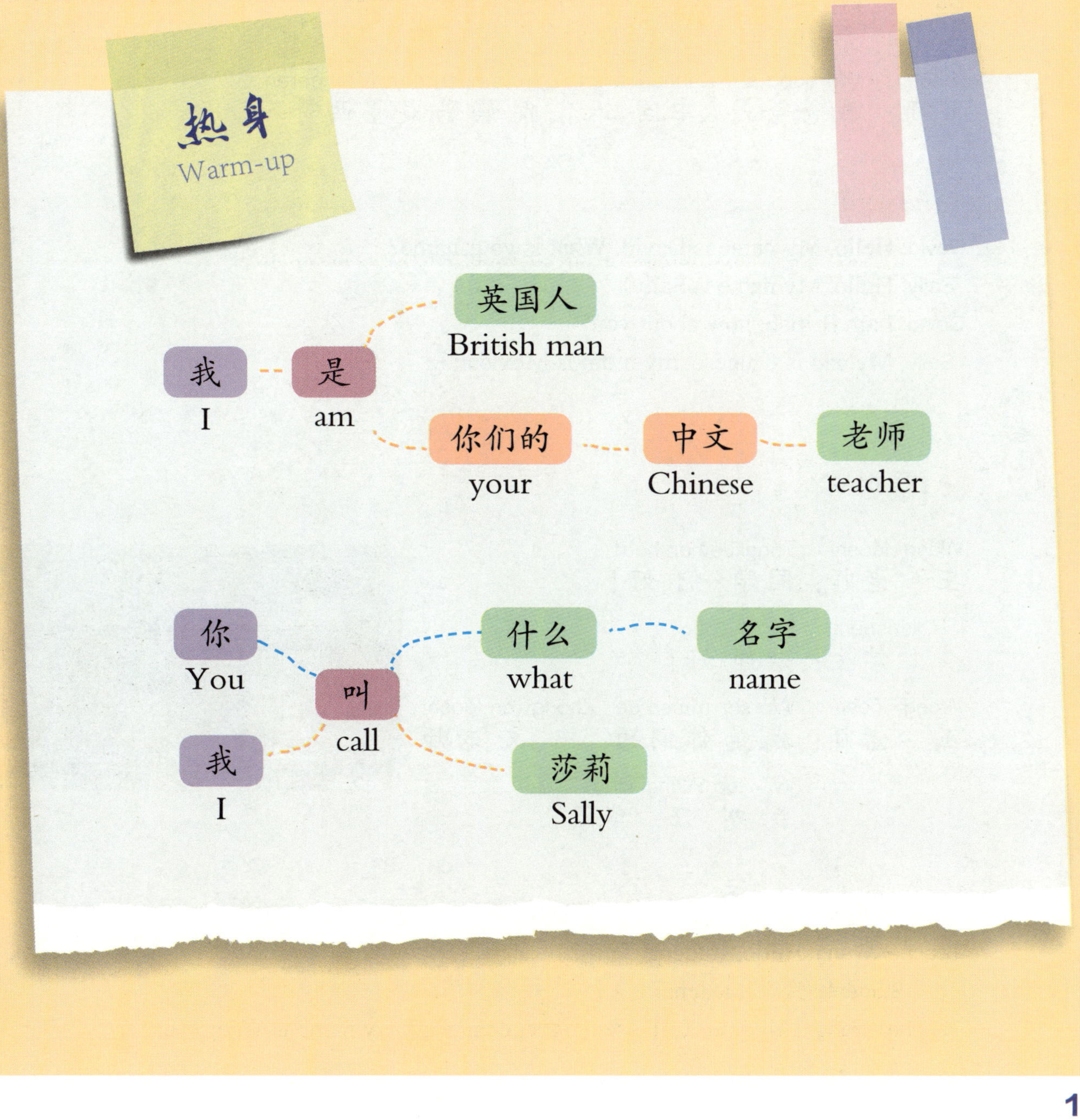

课文 Text

课文 1 01–1

Dàwèi: Nǐ hǎo. Wǒ jiào Dàwèi.
大卫：你好。我叫大卫。

Nǐ jiào shénme míngzi?
你叫什么名字？

Shālì: Nǐ hǎo. Wǒ jiào Shālì.
莎莉：你好。我叫莎莉。

Dàwèi: Wǒ shì Yīngguórén, nǐ ne?
大卫：我是英国人，你呢？

Shālì: Wǒ bàba shì Zhōngguórén, wǒ māma shì Mòxīgērén.
莎莉：我爸爸是中国人，我妈妈是墨西哥人。

Text One

David: Hello. My name is David. What is your name?

Sally: Hello. My name is Sally.

David: I am British, how about you?

Sally: My dad is Chinese, my mom is Mexican.

课文 2 01–2

Wáng lǎoshī: Tóngxuémen hǎo!
王老师：同学们好！

xuésheng: Lǎoshī hǎo!
学生：老师好！

Wáng lǎoshī: Wǒ shì nǐmen de Zhōngwén lǎoshī.
王老师：我是你们的中文老师。

Wǒ jiào Wáng Huá.
我叫王华。

Text Two

Teacher Wang: Hello, students!

Students: Hello, teacher!

Teacher Wang: I am your Chinese language teacher. My name is Wang Hua.

课文 3 01–3

Tā shì wǒ de Zhōngwén lǎoshī, tā de
她是我的中文老师，她的

míngzi jiào Wáng Huá. Tā shì wǒ de tóngxué,
名字叫王华。她是我的同学，

míngzi jiào Shālì, láizì Mòxīgē.
名字叫莎莉，来自墨西哥。

Text Three

She is my Chinese language teacher, and her name is Wang Hua. She is my classmate, her name is Sally, and she is from Mexico.

生词 New Words

你	nǐ	pron.	you (*sg.*)
好	hǎo	adj.	good
我	wǒ	pron.	I, me
叫	jiào	v.	to be called (a name), one's name is
什么	shénme	pron.	what
名字	míngzi	n.	name
是	shì	v.	to be
人	rén	n.	person, people
呢	ne	aux.	*used at the end of the sentence*
爸爸	bàba	n.	dad, father
妈妈	māma	n.	mom, mother
同学	tóngxué	n.	classmate
老师	lǎoshī	n.	teacher
你们	nǐmen	pron.	you (*pl.*)
的	de	part.	*used to indicate possession*
中文	Zhōngwén	n.	Chinese language
她	tā	pron.	she, her

专有名词 Proper Nouns

大卫	Dàwèi	David	英国人	Yīngguórén	British (person)
莎莉	Shālì	Sally	中国人	Zhōngguórén	Chinese (person)
王华	Wáng Huá	Wang Hua	墨西哥人	Mòxīgērén	Mexican (person)

语法点 Language Points

1 "叫"：中文里问别人名字的时候一般用"叫"，问"你叫什么名字"，回答"我叫王华"。如果是自我介绍，既可以说"我叫王华"，也可以说"我是王华"，前者强调自己的名字叫"王华"，不叫别的名字；后者强调自己是这个叫王华的人，不是别人。

"叫" (to be called a name/one's name is): in Chinese we usually use "叫" to ask for somebody's name. We may ask "你叫什么名字" (What is your name/What are you called) and answer "我叫王华" (My name is/I am called Wang Hua). When we introduce ourselves, we can choose to say either "我叫王华" (My name is/I am called Wang Hua) or "我是王华" (I am Wang Hua). The former emphasizes that I am called precisely "Wang Hua" and not a different name, whereas the latter emphasizes that I am this person called Wang Hua and not a different person.

2 疑问代词"什么"：可以直接做疑问句的宾语，也可与名词性词语一起做疑问句的宾语。例如：

The interrogative pronoun "什么": used in interrogative sentences, serving as the object either by itself or with a noun phrase following it. For example:

这是什么？

What is it?

你叫什么名字？

What is your name?

3 "是"字句：表示归类，主语所指事物是宾语所指事物的一部分。主语和宾语多为名词、代词。例如：

Sentences with "是" (to be): indicate a classification. The subject is a part of what the object indicates. The subject and the object are most often formed by nouns and pronouns.

For example:

我是英国人。

I am British (person).

我是你们的中文老师。

I am your Chinese language teacher.

她是我的同学。

She is my classmate.

4 “你呢”：“呢”用在名词或代词后构成疑问句，通常是根据上文的情况进行提问。例如：

“你呢” (How about you?/And you?) : “呢” is a particle used after a noun or a pronoun to form an interrogative sentence, and it’s usually based on the sentence preceding it. For example:

A: 你喜欢中文吗?

A: Do you like Chinese?

B: 我喜欢中文，你呢?

B: I like Chinese, how about you?

A: 我喜欢猫，你呢?

A: I like cats, how about you?

B: 我不喜欢猫，我喜欢狗。

B: I don't like cats, I like dogs.

5 结构助词“的”：名词 / 代词 + 的 + 名词，表示所属关系。如果“的”后面的名词是指人的名词或亲属称谓，可以省略“的”。例如：

The structural particle “的” : noun/pronoun + 的 + noun, indicates a relationship of possession or subordination. If “的” is followed by a noun indicating a person or kinship, we may omit “的”. For example:

他是我（的）老师。

He is my teacher.

他是我（的）同学。

He is my classmate.

她是我（的）妈妈。

She is my mom.

练习 Drills

听力练习 Listening Drills

1 听词语，判断图片是否正确。 01–4
Listen to the words and determine whether the pictures are correct.

(1) ____

(2) ____

(3) ____

(4) ____

(5) ____

2 听句子，选择正确图片。 01–5
Listen to the sentences and choose the correct pictures.

(1)

A

B

C

(2)

A

B

C

(3)

A

B

C

（4）

A B C

（5）

A B C

3 听对话，选择正确图片。 01–6

Listen to the conversations and choose the correct pictures.

A B C D E

（1）		（2）	
（3）		（4）	
（5）			

4 听录音，选择正确答案。 01–7

Listen to the recordings and choose the correct answers.

（1）A. 大卫 Dàwèi　B. 王 华 Wáng Huá　C. 莎莉 Shālì　（　　）

（2）A. 中 文 Zhōngwén　B. 英 国 Yīngguó　C. 同 学 tóngxué　（　　）

（3）A. 王 华 Wáng Huá　B. 莎莉 Shālì　C. 大卫 Dàwèi　（　　）

（4）A. 不是 bú shì　B. 是 shì　C. 墨西哥人 Mòxīgērén　（　　）

（5）A. 不是 bú shì　B. 老师 lǎoshī　C. 是 shì　（　　）

口语练习 Speaking Drills

5 听后重复。 01-8

Listen and repeat.

(1) ____________________

(2) ____________________

(3) ____________________

(4) ____________________

(5) ____________________

6 听后回答。 01-9

Listen and answer.

(1) ____________________

(2) ____________________

(3) ____________________

(4) ____________________

(5) ____________________

7 选词填空，读一读。

Fill in the blanks with the words and then read the text.

A. 的 (de)　　B. 叫 (jiào)　　C. 是 (shì)

Tā　wǒ de Zhōngwén lǎoshī, tā　míngzi jiào Wáng huá. Tā shì wǒ de tóngxué,
她（　）我的中文老师，她（　）名字叫王华。她是我的同学，

míngzi　Shālì, láizì Mòxīgē.
名字（　）莎莉，来自墨西哥。

2 Lesson Two

Tā jǐ suì le
她几岁了
How old is she

热身 Warm-up

她 She — 是 is — 你（的） your / 我（的） my — 女儿 daughter — 吗

小狗 Puppy — 现在 now — 多大 how old / 一岁零一个月 one year and one month — 了

课文 Text

课文 1 02–1

Shālì: Lǎoshī, tā shì nín nǚ'ér ma?
莎莉：老师，她是您女儿吗？

Wáng lǎoshī: Shì de, tā shì wǒ nǚ'ér.
王 老师：是的，她是我女儿。

Shālì: Tā jiào shénme míngzi? Jǐ suì le?
莎莉：她叫什么名字？几岁了？

Wáng lǎoshī: Tā jiào Xiǎopíngguǒ, jīnnián sān suì.
王 老师：她叫小苹果，今年三岁。

Text One

Sally: Teacher, is she your daughter?
Teacher Wang: Yes, she is my daughter.
Sally: What's her name? How old is she?
Teacher Wang: Her name is Xiaopingguo. She is three years old.

课文 2 02–2

Shālì: Lǎoshī, zhè shì nín jiā de xiǎo gǒu ma?
莎莉：老师，这是您家的小狗吗？

Wáng lǎoshī: Shì de.
王 老师：是的。

Shālì: Xiǎo gǒu jiào shénme míngzi?
莎莉：小狗叫什么名字？

Wáng lǎoshī: Jiào Diǎndian.
王 老师：叫点点。

Shālì: Diǎndian xiànzài duō dà le?
莎莉：点点现在多大了？

Wáng lǎoshī: Yí suì líng yí gè yuè.
王 老师：一岁零一个月。

Text Two

Sally: Teacher, is this your family's puppy?
Teacher Wang: Yes.
Sally: What's the puppy's name?
Teacher Wang: It's called Diandian.
Sally: How old is Diandian now?
Teacher Wang: One year and one month old.

课文 3 02–3

Wáng lǎoshī jīnnián sānshí suì. Tā nǚ'ér
王 老师 今年 三十 岁。她 女儿
jīnnián sān suì, míngzi jiào Xiǎopíngguǒ,
今年 三 岁，名字 叫 小 苹 果，
hěn piàoliang. Lǎoshī jiā de xiǎo gǒu míngzi
很 漂亮 。老师 家的 小 狗 名字
jiào Diǎndian, xiànzài yí suì líng yí gè yuè.
叫 点点 ，现在 一岁 零一个 月。

Text Three

Teacher Wang is thirty years old this year. Her daughter is three years old this year, her name is Xiaopingguo, and she is very pretty. Their puppy is called Diandian, and it's one year and one month old now.

生词 New Words

您	nín	pron.	you (*polite form*)	女儿	nǚ'ér	n.	daughter
几	jǐ	pron.	how many	岁	suì	n.	years (of age)
了	le	part.	*used at the end of or in the middle of a sentence, to indicate a change or a new circumstance*	小	xiǎo	adj.	small, little
苹果	píngguǒ	n.	apple	今年	jīnnián	n.	this year
三	sān	num.	three	这	zhè	pron.	this
家	jiā	n.	family, home	狗	gǒu	n.	dog

续表

吗	ma	part.	*used at the end of a question*	现在	xiànzài	n.	now
多	duō	adj.	many, much	大	dà	adj.	big
一	yī	num.	one	零	líng	num.	zero
个	gè	m.	*measure word*	月	yuè	n.	month
三十	sānshí	num.	thirty	很	hěn	adv.	very
漂亮	piàoliang	adj.	pretty, beautiful				

专有名词 Proper Nouns

点点	Diǎndian	Diandian

语法点 Language Points

1 名词谓语句：是名词性成分作谓语的句子，主要用来说明年龄、时间等。例如：

Noun-predicate sentences: sentences in which the predicate is formed by a noun or a noun construction. They're mainly used to express age, time, etc. For example:

我今年三十岁。（表示年龄）

I am 30 years old this year. (expresses age)

今天星期一。（表示时间）

It is Monday today. (expresses time)

这本书二十块钱。

This book is 20 dollars.

他英国人，我墨西哥人。

He is British, and I am Mexican.

2 语气助词"了"：用在句子末尾，表示变化或出现新情况。例如：

The modal particle "了": used at the end of a sentence to express a change or a new situation. For example:

你今年多大了？

How old are you this year?

我今年三十岁了。

I am 30 years old this year.

我看见你了。

I saw you.

3 “几岁”和“多大”：“几岁”和“多大”都可以问年龄。“几岁”多用于问 10 岁以下的孩子。例如：

“几岁” and “多大” : “几岁” and “多大” are both used to inquire one’s age. “几岁” is mainly used to ask the age of children under 10 years old. For example:

A：你女儿几岁了？

A：How old is your daughter?

B：我女儿三岁了。

B：My daughter is three years old.

“多大”可以问孩子，也可以问成人。例如：

“多大” can be used to ask the age of both children and adults. For example:

A：你女儿多大了？

A：How old is your daughter?

B：我女儿四个月了。

B：My daughter is four months old.

另外，动物也有年龄。对幼小的动物，可以用“多大”或“几个月”；对成年的动物，用“几岁”。

Moreover, animals also have an age. For young animals, we can use “多大” or “几个月”; for adult animals, we use “几岁”.

4 “零”：放在两个数量中间，表示比较大的量之下附有比较小的量。例如：

“零”(zero) : is placed between two amounts/numbers, to show that there is a smaller amount/number attached to the larger one. For example:

我来北京一年零一个月了。

I’ve been in Beijing for one year and one month.

他女儿今年一岁零一个月了。

His daughter is one year and one month old this year.

5 形容词谓语句：中文里形容词可以直接做句子的谓语。例如：

Adjective-predicate sentences: in Chinese, adjectives can directly function as predicates. For example:

她女儿很漂亮。
Her daughter is very pretty.
我的朋友很漂亮。
My friend is very pretty.

注意：形容词前常常有“很”。
Note: “很” is commonly placed in front of adjectives.

练习 Drills

听力练习 Listening Drills

1 听词语，判断图片是否正确。 02-4
Listen to the words and determine whether the pictures are correct.

(1) ______

(2) ______

(3) ______

(4) ______

(5) ______

2 听句子，选择正确图片。 02-5
Listen to the sentences and choose the correct pictures.

(1)

A

B

C

(2)

A

B

C

（3）

A B C

（4）

A B C

（5）

A B C

3 听对话，选择正确图片。 02–6

Listen to the conversations and choose the correct pictures.

（1）		（2）	
（3）		（4）	
（5）			

4 听录音，选择正确答案。 02–7

Listen to the recordings and choose the correct answers.

（1）A. 一岁 (yí suì)　　B. 三岁 (sān suì)　　C. 四岁 (sì suì)　　（　　）

（2）A. 不漂亮 (bú piàoliang)　　B. 三岁了 (sān suì le)　　C. 很漂亮 (hěn piàoliang)　　（　　）

（3）A. Diǎndian 点点　　B. xiǎo gǒu 小狗　　C. tā de 她的　　（　　）

（4）A. sānshí suì 三十岁　　B. sān suì 三岁　　C. sān gè yuè 三个月　　（　　）

（5）A. yí suì líng sān gè yuè 一岁零三个月　　B. yí suì líng yí gè yuè 一岁零一个月

C. yí suì líng sì gè yuè 一岁零四个月　　（　　）

口语练习 Speaking Drills

5 听后重复。 02-8

Listen and repeat.

（1）____________________________

（2）____________________________

（3）____________________________

（4）____________________________

（5）____________________________

6 听后回答。 02-9

Listen and answer.

（1）____________________________

（2）____________________________

（3）____________________________

（4）____________________________

（5）____________________________

7 回答问题。

Answer the question.

Mófǎng kèwén nèiróng, jièshào yí gè nǐ de péngyou. míngzi niánlíng děng
模仿课文内容，介绍一个你的朋友。（名字、年龄等）

Using the text as reference, introduce a friend of yours. (name, age, etc.)

____

____

3 Lesson Three

Tā huì xiě hěn duō Hànzì

她会写很多汉字

She can write many Chinese characters

热身 Warm-up

你的 Your — 名字 name — 怎么 how — 读 read / 写 write

你 You / 我 I — 不 not — 会 can — 做 do — 中国菜 Chinese food — 吗

课文 Text

课文 1 03-1

Dàwèi: Nǐ de Zhōngwén míngzi zěnme dú?
大卫：你的中文名字怎么读？

Shālì:
莎莉：Sh-ā l-ì.

Dàwèi: Hànzì zěnme xiě? Duìbuqǐ, hěn duō zì wǒ bú huì xiě.
大卫：汉字怎么写？对不起，很多字我不会写。

Shālì: Méi guānxi. Nǐ kàn, shì zhème xiě.
莎莉：没关系。你看，是这么写。

Text One

David: How do you pronounce your Chinese name?

Sally: Sh-ā l-ì.

David: How do you write the Chinese characters for your name? I'm sorry, there are many characters I can't write.

Sally: No problem. Look, this is how you write them.

课文 2 03-2

Dàwèi: Zhège Zhōngwén zěnme shuō?
大卫：这个中文怎么说？

Shālì: Shì Zhōngguó cài.
莎莉：是中国菜。

Dàwèi: Nǐ huì zuò Zhōngguó cài ma?
大卫：你会做中国菜吗？

Shālì: Wǒ bú huì zuò, wǒ māma huì zuò.
莎莉：我不会做，我妈妈会做。

Text Two

David: How do you say this in Chinese?

Sally: It's Chinese food.

David: Can you make Chinese food?

Sally: I can't, but my mom can.

课文 3 03–3

Hěn duō Hànzì wǒ huì dú bú huì xiě. Jīntiān
很多汉字我会读不会写。今天
wǒ huì xiě Shālì de míngzi le. Shālì de
我会写莎莉的名字了。莎莉的
Zhōngwén hěn hǎo, tā huì xiě hěn duō Hànzì.
中文很好，她会写很多汉字。

Text Three

There are many Chinese characters I can read but cannot write. Today I am able to write Sally's name. Sally's Chinese is very good, and she can write many Chinese characters.

生词 New Words

怎么	zěnme	pron.	how
读	dú	v.	to read, to pronounce
汉字	Hànzì	n.	Chinese character, Hanzi
写	xiě	v.	to write
对不起	duìbuqǐ	v.	I'm sorry
字	zì	n.	character, written word
会	huì	v.	can, to be able to
没关系	méi guānxi		no problem
看	kàn	v.	to look, to see
这么	zhème	adv.	this is how…, this way
说	shuō	v.	to say
中国菜	Zhōngguó cài	n.	Chinese food/dishes
做	zuò	v.	to do, to make
今天	jīntiān	n.	today

语法点 Language Points

1 “怎么” + 动词：询问动作的方式。例如：

“怎么”+ verb : used to inquire the manner of the action. For example:

你的名字怎么写？

How do you write your name?

中国菜怎么做？

How do you make Chinese food?

这个字怎么读？

How do you pronounce this character?

2 能愿动词“会”：用在动词前，表示通过学习可以获得的能力。例如：

The modal verb “会” : used before a verb to indicate an ability obtained through learning. For example:

我会说中文。

I can speak Chinese.

我会写很多汉字。

I can write many Chinese characters.

3 主谓谓语句：主谓短语做谓语的句子，主句主语在意念上是谓语里的一个成分。例如：

Subject-predicate predicate sentences: sentences in which the subject-predicate phrase serves as the predicate; the subject of the main sentence is a part of the predicate. For example:

很多汉字	我	会读不会写。
这个字	我	不会读。
这个菜	我	不会做。
subject1	predicate1	
	subject2	predicate2

4 “这么” + 动词：指示方式。例如：

“这么”+verb : indicates the manner. For example:

我的名字这么写。

This is how you write my name.

这个字这么读。

This is how you pronounce this character.

这个东西这么吃。

This is how you eat this thing.

练习 Drills

听力练习 Listening Drills

1 听词语，判断图片是否正确。 03-4

Listen to the words and determine whether the pictures are correct.

____ ____ ____ ____ ____

2 听句子，选择正确图片。 03-5

Listen to the sentences and choose the correct pictures.

(1)

A

B

C

(2)

A

B

C

（3）

A

B

C

（4）

A

B

C

（5）

A

B

C

3 听对话，选择正确图片。 03-6

Listen to the conversations and choose the correct pictures.

A

B

C

D

E

（1）		（2）	
（3）		（4）	
（5）			

4 听录音，选择正确答案。 03-7

Listen to the recordings and choose the correct answers.

(1)	A. huì xiě 会写	B. bú huì xiě 不会写	C. huì dú 会读	( )
(2)	A. Zhōngguó cài 中国菜	B. Zhōngguó 中国	C. hěn xǐhuan 很喜欢	( )
(3)	A. Shālì 莎莉	B. Shālí 莎莉	C. Shàlí 莎莉	( )
(4)	A. yí suì 一岁	B. bú huì 不会	C. sì suì 四岁	( )
(5)	A. mǐfàn 米饭	B. qù Zhōngguó 去中国	C. Zhōngguó cài 中国菜	( )

口语练习 Speaking Drills

5 听后重复。 03-8

Listen and repeat.

(1) ______

(2) ______

(3) ______

(4) ______

(5) ______

6 听后回答。 03-9

Listen and answer.

(1) ______

(2) ______

(3) ______

(4) ______

(5) ______

7 选词填空，读一读。
Fill in the blanks with the words and then read the text.

duō　　huì　　jīn tiān　　le　　de
A. 多　B. 会　C. 今天　D. 了　E. 的

Hànzì hěn duō. Hěn (　　) Hànzì wǒ (　　) dú bú (　　) xiě. (　　) wǒ huì xiě Shālì de míngzi (　　). Shālì (　　) Zhōngwén hěn hǎo, tā huì xiě hěn duō Hànzì.
汉字很多。很（　　）汉字我（　　）读不（　　）写。（　　）我会写莎莉的名字（　　）。莎莉（　　）中文很好，她会写很多汉字。

4 Lesson Four

Zhōngwǔ nǐ xiǎng chī shénme

中午你想吃什么

What do you want to eat for lunch

热身 Warm-up

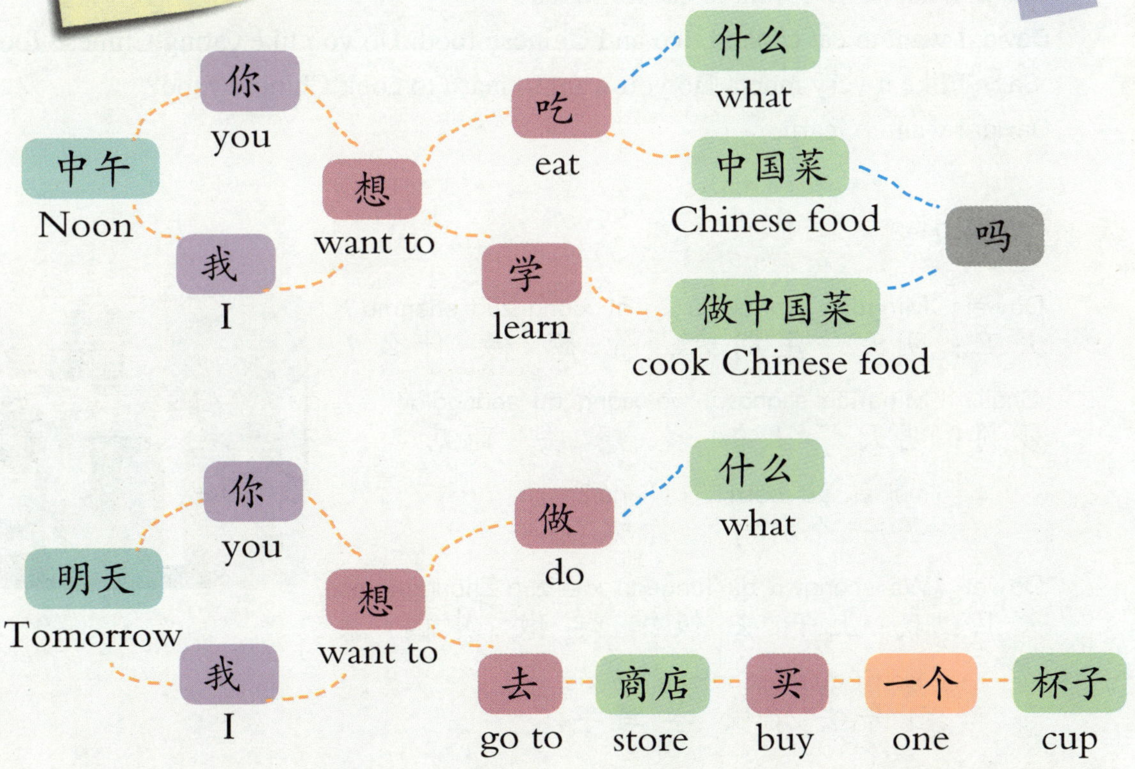

课文 Text

课文 1 04-1

Shālì: Zhōngwǔ nǐ xiǎng chī shénme?
莎莉：中午你想吃什么？

Dàwèi: Wǒ xiǎng chī mǐfàn hé Zhōngguó cài.
大卫：我想吃米饭和中国菜。

Nǐ ài chī Zhōngguó cài ma?
你爱吃中国菜吗？

Shālì: Wǒ hěn ài chī. Nǐ xiǎng xué zuò Zhōngguó cài ma?
莎莉：我很爱吃。你想学做中国菜吗？

Dàwèi: Wǒ xiǎng xué.
大卫：我想学。

Text One

Sally: What do you want to eat for lunch?

David: I want to eat cooked rice and Chinese food. Do you like eating Chinese food?

Sally: I like it very much. Do you want to learn to cook Chinese food?

David: I want to learn.

课文 2 04-2

Dàwèi: Míngtiān xīngqī liù, nǐ xiǎng zuò shénme?
大卫：明天星期六，你想做什么？

Shālì: Míngtiān shàngwǔ wǒ xiǎng qù shāngdiàn
莎莉：明天上午我想去商店

mǎi yí gè bēizi. Nǐ ne?
买一个杯子。你呢？

Dàwèi: Wǒ shàngwǔ qù fànguǎn xué zuò Zhōngguó cài,
大卫：我上午去饭馆学做中国菜，

xiàwǔ qù xuéxiào xué xiě zì.
下午去学校学写字。

Text Two

David: It is Saturday tomorrow. What do you want to do?

Sally: I want to go to the store to buy a cup tomorrow morning. How about you?

David: In the morning I'm going to the restaurant to learn to cook Chinese food, and in the afternoon I'm going to school to learn to write Hanzi.

课文 3 04–3

Míngtiān xīngqī liù . Shālì xiǎng qù shāngdiàn
明天 星期六。莎莉 想 去 商店

mǎi bēizi . Wǒ xiǎng shàngwǔ qù fànguǎn xué
买 杯子。我 想 上午 去 饭馆 学

zuò Zhōngguó cài , xiàwǔ qù xuéxiào xué xiě zì .
做 中国 菜，下午 去 学校 学 写 字。

Text Three

Tomorrow is Saturday. Sally wants to go to the store to buy a cup. I want to go to the restaurant in the morning to learn to cook Chinese food and to the school in the afternoon to learn to write Hanzi.

生词 New Words

中午	zhōngwǔ	n.	noon
想	xiǎng	v./mod.	to want, to miss
吃	chī	v.	to eat
米饭	mǐfàn	n.	cooked rice
爱	ài	v.	to like, to love
学	xué	v.	to learn
明天	míngtiān	n.	tomorrow
星期六	xīngqī liù	n.	Saturday
去	qù	v.	to go
商店	shāngdiàn	n.	store, shop
买	mǎi	v.	to buy
杯子	bēizi	n.	cup, glass
上午	shàngwǔ	n.	morning
饭馆	fànguǎn	n.	restaurant
下午	xiàwǔ	n.	afternoon
学校	xuéxiào	n.	school

语法点 Language Points

1 连动句：一个句子有两个或两个以上的动词，后一个动作是前一个动作的目的。例如：

Sentences with serial verb phrases: in sentences with two or more verbs, the latter action is the purpose of the former action. For example:

我去商店买杯子。

I am going to the store to buy a cup.

我去饭馆吃中国菜。

I am going to the restaurant to eat Chinese food.

这种句子都可以拆分为两个句子。例如：

This type of sentence can always be split into two sentences. For example:

我去商店买杯子。——我去商店；我买杯子（商店里有杯子）。

I am going to the store to buy a cup.——I go to the store; I buy a cup (there are cups at the store).

我去饭馆吃中国菜。——我去饭馆；我吃中国菜（饭馆里有菜）。

I am going to the restaurant to eat Chinese food. ——I go to the restaurant; I eat Chinese food (there is food at the restaurant).

注意：这种句子动词的顺序不能颠倒，句子中间也没有语音停顿。

Note: The order of the verbs in this type of sentence cannot be reversed and there is no pause in the middle of the sentence.

2 时间名词的位置：中文时间名词可以放在主语的前面或后面表示时间。例如：

Position of time nouns: time nouns in Chinese can be placed in front of the subject or after the subject to express the time. For example:

我明天去商店。

[I tomorrow go to the shop] I will go to the shop tomorrow.

明天我去商店。

[Tomorrow I go to the shop] I will go to the shop tomorrow.

3 能愿动词“想”：用在动词前，表示要做某事的意愿，可以用程度副词修饰。

例如：

The modal verb "想" : used in front of the verb to express the wish to do something; it can be modified by an adverb of degree. For example:

我想去北京。

I want to go to Beijing.

我想吃中国菜。

I want to eat Chinese food.

我很想学做中国菜。

[I very want learn make Chinese food] I want to learn to make Chinese food very much.

练习 Drills

听力练习 Listening Drills

1 听词语，判断图片是否正确。 04–4

Listen to the words and determine whether the pictures are correct.

____ ____ ____ ____ ____

2 听句子，选择正确图片。 04–5

Listen to the sentences and choose the correct pictures.

(1)

A B C

（2）

A　　B　　C

（3）

A　　B　　C

（4）

A　　B　　C

（5）

A　　B　　C

3 听对话，选择正确图片。 04-6
Listen to the conversations and choose the correct pictures.

（1）		（2）	
（3）		（4）	
（5）			

4 听录音，选择正确答案。 04–7
Listen to the recordings and choose the correct answers.

	A	B	C	
(1)	Zhōngguó cài 中国菜	píngguǒ 苹果	mǐfàn 米饭	(　　)
(2)	shāngdiàn 商店	xuéxiào 学校	bēizi 杯子	(　　)
(3)	xué zuò mǐfàn 学做米饭	xué zuò Zhōngguó cài 学做中国菜	qù fànguǎn 去饭馆	(　　)
(4)	qù xuéxiào 去学校	mǎi dōngxi 买东西	xué xiě zì 学写字	(　　)
(5)	míngtiān zhōngwǔ 明天中午	xīngqī liù zhōngwǔ 星期六中午	xīngqī liù xiàwǔ 星期六下午	(　　)

口语练习 Speaking Drills

5 听后重复。 04–8
Listen and repeat.

(1) ______________________

(2) ______________________

(3) ______________________

(4) ______________________

(5) ______________________

6 听后回答。 04–9
Listen and answer.

(1) ______________________

(2) ______________________

(3) ______________________

(4) ______________________

(5) ______________________

7 回答问题。

Answer the question.

Mófǎng kèwén nèiróng, shuōshuo nǐ xīngqī liù de jìhuà.
模仿 课文 内容，说说 你星期六的计划。

Using the text as reference, talk about your plans for Saturday.

5 Lesson Five

Duōshao qián yí gè

多少钱一个

How much does one cost

热身 Warm-up

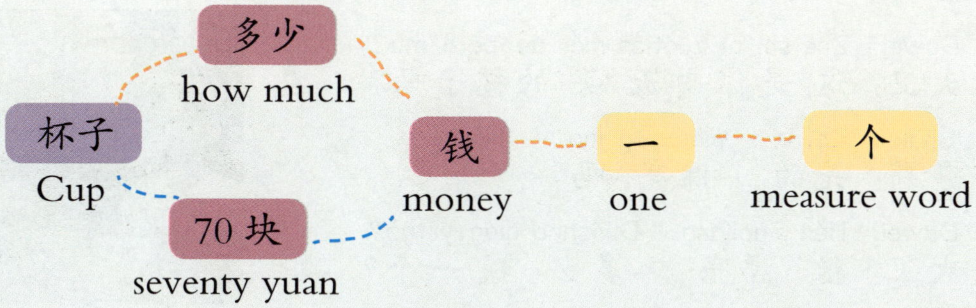

课文 Text

课文 1 05-1

chūzūchē sījī: Nǐ hǎo. Nǐ qù nǎr?
出租车司机：你好。你去哪儿？

Shālì: Nǐ hǎo. Wǒ qù Tiāntiān shāngdiàn.
莎莉：你好。我去天天商店。

Shālì: Nǐ hǎo. Duōshao qián?
莎莉：你好。多少钱？

chūzūchē sījī: Èrshí kuài qián. Xièxie!
出租车司机：二十块钱。谢谢！

Text One

Taxi driver: Hello. Where are you going?
Sally: Hello. I am going to Tiantian store.

Sally: Hi, how much does it cost?
Taxi driver: Twenty yuan. Thank you!

课文 2 05-2

Dàwèi: Zhè shì nǐ zuótiān mǎi de bēizi ma?
大卫：这是你昨天买的杯子吗？

Shālì: Shì de, piàoliang ma?
莎莉：是的，漂亮吗？

Dàwèi: Hěn piàoliang. Duōshao qián yí gè?
大卫：很漂亮。多少钱一个？

Shālì: Qīshí kuài qián yí gè. Nǐ xiǎng mǎi yí gè ma?
莎莉：七十块钱一个。你想买一个吗？

Dàwèi: Wǒ bù mǎi, wǒ yǒu bēizi.
大卫：我不买，我有杯子。

Text Two

David: Is this the cup you bought yesterday?
Sally: Yes, isn't it pretty?
David: Very pretty. How much does it cost?
David: Seventy yuan for one. Do you want to buy one?
Sally: No, I have one.

课文 3 05-3

Shālì de bēizi hěn piàoliang, qīshí kuài qián yí gè. Tā mǎile sān gè, tā yí gè, tā bàba yí gè, tā māma yí gè.
莎莉的杯子很漂亮，七十块钱一个。她买了三个，她一个，她爸爸一个，她妈妈一个。

Text Three

Sally's cup is very pretty, and it cost 70 yuan. She bought three, one for herself, one for her dad and one for her mom.

生词 New Words

哪儿	nǎr	pron.	where (*question*)
多少	duōshao	pron.	how much
钱	qián	n.	money
二十	èrshí	num.	twenty
块	kuài	m.	*kuai* (spoken version of *yuan,* the basic unit of money in China)
谢谢	xièxie	v.	thank you
昨天	zuótiān	n.	yesterday
七十	qīshí	num.	seventy
不	bù	adv.	no, not
有	yǒu	v.	to have, to exist

语法点 Language Points

1 “多少钱”：（1）询问东西的价格。例如：
“多少钱” (How much does it cost): (1) used to inquire the price of things. For example:
这个杯子多少钱？
How much does this cup cost?

（2）询问做某事的花费。例如：

Used to inquire the cost of doing something. For example:

坐出租车去火车站多少钱？

How much does it cost to take a taxi to the railway station?

坐飞机去中国多少钱？

How much does it cost to fly to China?

“多少”是疑问代词，询问十以上的数量。“多少 +（量词）+ 名词”，中间的量词有时可以省略。例如：

“多少” is an interrogative pronoun used to inquire about quantities higher than 10. The construction used is “多少 + (measure word) + noun” ; in some situations the measure word in the middle can be omitted. For example:

一个月多少天？

How many days are there in a month?

你写了多少（个）字？

How many characters did you write?

2 “了”：“了”放在动词后，“动词 + 了 + 宾语”，表示动作完成。例如：

“了” : “了” is placed after the verb and the construction “verb + 了 + object” expresses a completed action. For example:

她买了三个杯子。

She bought three cups.

昨天我买了五个苹果。

Yesterday I bought five apples.

今天上午我吃了两个苹果。

This morning I ate two apples.

3 “有”：动词，主语是人时，表示“拥有”。例如：

“有” : verb, when the subject is a person, it expresses possession. For example:

我有一个杯子。

I have a cup.

我有一本中文书。

I have a Chinese book.

否定式为“没有 + 名词”。例如：

The negative form is “没有+ noun”. For example:

我没有杯子。

I don’t have a cup.

我没有中文书。

I don’t have a Chinese book.

注意：肯定句里一般有数量词，否定句里一般不出现数量词。

Note: Affirmative sentences usually use a quantifier, whereas negative sentences usually don’t.

4 疑问代词“哪儿”：询问处所。例如：

The interrogative pronoun “哪儿” : used to inquire the place or location. For example:

你去哪儿？

Where are you going?

你想去哪儿吃饭？

Where do you want to go to eat?

你去哪儿买苹果？

Where do you go to buy apples?

5 钱数的表达：人民币的常用单位是“元”“角”，口语里分别用“块”“毛”表示，后面还常常加上“钱”字。例如：

Expressing an amount of money: The common units of RMB are “元” and “角”, but in spoken Chinese, people say “块” and “毛” instead, followed by the word “钱”. For example:

这个杯子七十块钱一个。

This cup costs 70 yuan.

这个苹果五块钱一个。

This apple costs five yuan.

这本书五十块钱。

This book costs 50 yuan.

练习 Drills

听力练习 Listening Drills

1 听词语，判断图片是否正确。 05–4
Listen to the words and determine whether the pictures are correct.

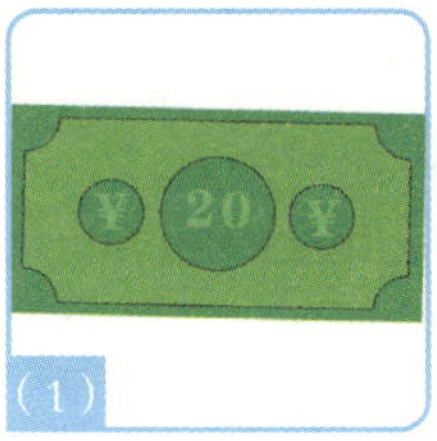

(1) ____

(2) ____

(3) ____

(4) ____

(5) ____

2 听句子，选择正确图片。 05–5
Listen to the sentences and choose the correct pictures.

(1)

A

B

C

(2)

A

B

C

(3)

A

B

C

(4)

A

B

C

(5)

A

B

C

3 听对话，选择正确图片。 05-6

Listen to the conversations and choose the correct pictures.

A

B

C

D

E

(1)		(2)	
(3)		(4)	
(5)			

4 听录音，选择正确答案。 05-7

Listen to the recordings and choose the correct answers.

(1) A. 一个 杯子 (yí gè bēizi)　B. 三 个 苹 果 (sān gè píngguǒ)　C. 三 个 杯子 (sān gè bēizi)　(　　)

(2) A. 一个 (yí gè)　B. 三 个 (sān gè)　C. 四个 (sì gè)　(　　)

(3) A. 五十 块 钱 (wǔshí kuài qián)　B. 七十 块 钱 (qīshí kuài qián)　C. 九十 块 钱 (jiǔshí kuài qián)　(　　)

(4) A. 天 天 商 店 (Tiāntiān shāngdiàn)　B. 她不去 (tā bú qù)　C. 她去 学 校 (tā qù xuéxiào)　(　　)

(5) A. 想 买 杯子 (xiǎng mǎi bēizi)　B. 不 想 买 杯子 (bù xiǎng mǎi bēizi)　C. 想 买 苹 果 (xiǎng mǎi píngguǒ)　(　　)

口语练习 Speaking Drills

5 听后重复。 05-8

Listen and repeat.

(1) ______

(2) ______

(3) ______

(4) ______

(5) ______

6 听后回答。 05-9

Listen and answer.

(1) ______

(2) ______

(3) ______

(4) ______

(5) ______

7 回答问题。

Answer the question.

Mófǎng kèwén, shuōshuo māma zuótiān mǎile shénme.
模仿 课文， 说说 妈妈 昨天 买 了 什么。

Using the text as reference, talk about what mother bought yesterday.

______

______

6 Lesson Six

Zhèxiē píngguǒ shang yǒu zì

这些苹果上有字

There are words written on these apples

热身 Warm-up

这些 These — 苹果 apple — 上 on — 有 — 字 character

我们（的） Our — 学校 university — 里 in — 有 — 医院 hospital

课文 Text

课文 1 06–1

Dàwèi: Nǐ hǎo. Píngguǒ zài nǎr?
大卫：你好。苹果在哪儿？

shòuhuòyuán: Píngguǒ zài nàr.
售货员：苹果在那儿。

Dàwèi: Zhèxiē píngguǒ shang yǒu zì.
大卫：这些苹果上有字。

Zhège zì shì "ài".
这个字是"爱"。

Nàge zì shì shénme?
那个字是什么？

shòuhuòyuán: Nàge zì dú "xǐ".
售货员：那个字读"囍"。

Text One

David: Hello. Where are the apples?
Shop assistant: The apples are over there.
David: There are characters on these apples. This character is "爱" (ài, love). What is that character?
Shop assistant: That character is pronounced "囍"(xǐ, double happiness).

课文 2 06–2

Dàwèi: Lǎoshī, wǒmen xuéxiào li yǒu yīyuàn ma?
大卫：老师，我们学校里有医院吗？

Wáng lǎoshī: Yǒu.
王老师：有。

Dàwèi: Xuéxiào de yīyuàn zài nǎr?
大卫：学校的医院在哪儿？

Wáng lǎoshī: Zài shuǐguǒ shāngdiàn hòumiàn. Zěnme le?
王老师：在水果商店后面。怎么了？

Dàwèi: Wǒ de péngyou xiǎng qù kàn yīshēng.
大卫：我的朋友想去看医生。

Text Two

David: Teacher, is there a hospital in our university (campus)?
Teacher Wang: There is one.
David: Where is the university hospital?
Teacher Wang: It's behind the fruit shop. What happened?
David: My friend wants to go see a doctor.

课文 3 06–3

Wǒmen xuéxiào li yǒu yí gè hěn dà de shuǐguǒ
我们 学校 里 有 一 个 很 大 的 水果

shāngdiàn. Hěn duō xuéshēng zài nàr mǎi dōngxi.
商店。很 多 学生 在 那儿 买 东西。

Jīntiān zhōngwǔ wǒ qù shāngdiàn mǎile yìxiē
今天 中午 我 去 商店 买了 一些

píngguǒ. Zhèxiē píngguǒ shang yǒu zì, yí gè
苹果。这些 苹果 上 有 字，一 个

shì "ài" zì, yí gè shì "xǐ" zì.
是"爱"字，一 个 是"囍"字。

Text Three

There is a big fruit shop inside our university (campus). Many students go there to buy things. At noon today I went to the shop and bought some apples. These apples have characters written on them: one of them is the "爱" character, the other one is the "囍" character.

生词 New Words

在	zài	v./prep.	to be at/in/on
那儿	nàr	pron.	there
些	xiē	m.	some
上	shang	n.	on (*used after the noun*)
我们	wǒmen	pron.	we, us

续表

里	li	n.	inside (*used after the noun*)
医院	yīyuàn	n.	hospital
水果	shuǐguǒ	n.	fruit
后面	hòumiàn	n.	behind (*used after the noun*)
朋友	péngyou	n.	friend
医生	yīshēng	n.	doctor
学生	xuésheng	n.	student

语法点 Language Points

1 动词"在": 后面加表示位置的名词或代词,表示什么人或事物在什么地方。例如:

The verb"在" : followed by nouns or pronouns which indicate a place or position, used to express where someone or something is. For example:

苹果在哪儿? 苹果在那儿。

Where are the apples? The apples are there.

我在家。

I am at home.

莎莉在商店。

Sally is at the shop.

2 "那儿" : 指代处所，多用于口语。例如:

"那儿" : indicates a location, mainly used in oral Chinese. For example:

苹果在那儿。

The apples are there.

大卫在那儿。

David is there.

电视在那儿。

The TV is there.

3 "有" : 表示存在，某处存在某人或某物。例如:

"有" : expresses the existence of someone or something in some place. For example:

那个商店有很多水果。

There are many fruits at that store.

我们学校里有一个医院。

There is a hospital in our school.

那个饭馆有很多人。

There are many people at that restaurant.

4 “怎么了”：常用于对听到的或看到的情况产生疑问时，意思是“发生了什么事儿？你为什么这么说？”。例如：

“怎么了”: is often used to express a question someone has towards something they saw or heard, meaning “What happened? Why do you say that?”. For example:

A：学校里有医院吗？

A：Is there a hospital in the university?

B：有。怎么了？

B：There is. What happened?

A：饭馆里有电视吗？

A：Is there a TV in the restaurant?

B：没有。怎么了？

B：There is not. Why do you ask that?

5 “一个……一个”：中文里表示列举的时候，如果列举的事物是两个或三个，为了突出每一个的特点，可以用“一个……一个……（一个）”。例如：

“一个……一个”: The construction used when enumerating things in Chinese, if there are two or three things to enumerate, we can use the construction “一个……一个……(一个)” to emphasize each of these things. For example:

我有两个名字，一个是大卫，一个是 David。

I have two names. One is 大卫, the other one is David.

我有三个朋友，一个在英国，一个在中国，一个在墨西哥。

I have three friends. One is in the UK, one is in China, and the other one is in Mexico.

6 方位词“上”“里”：“上”“里”用在名词后读轻声。例如：

The nouns of locality “上” “里”: “上” and “里” are pronounced on a neutral tone when used after nouns. For example:

桌子上有一本书。
There is a book on the table.
苹果上有一个字。
There is a character on the apple.

椅子上有水。
There is water on the chair.
商店里有很多人。
There are many people in the store.

练习 Drills

听力练习 Listening Drills

1 听词语，判断图片是否正确。 06-4
Listen to the words and determine whether the pictures are correct.

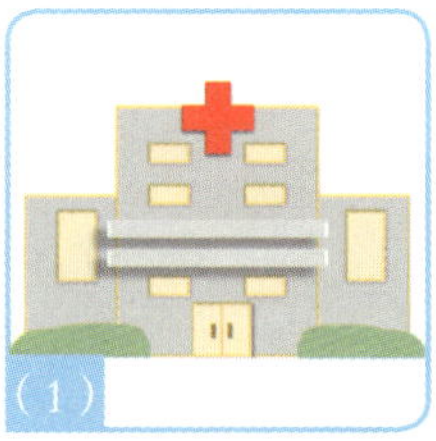
(1) ____

(2) ____

(3) ____

(4) ____

(5) ____

2 听句子，选择正确图片。 06-5
Listen to the sentences and choose the correct pictures.

(1)

A

B

C

(2)

A

B

C

(3)

A　　B　　C

(4)

A　　B　　C

(5)

A　　B　　C

3 听对话，选择正确图片。 06–6
Listen to the conversations and choose the correct pictures.

(1)		(2)	
(3)		(4)	
(5)			

4 听录音，选择正确答案。 06–7
Listen to the recordings and choose the correct answers.

(1) A. yǒu zì 有字　　B. yǒu rén 有人　　C. yǒu shuǐ 有水　　(　　)

(2)	A. zài shāngdiàn 在 商 店	B. zài xuéxiào 在 学 校	C. zài jiā 在 家	( )
(3)	A. diànshì 电 视	B. Zhōngwén shū 中 文 书	C. píngguǒ 苹 果	( )
(4)	A. yǒu píngguǒ 有 苹 果	B. yǒu xǐ zì 有 "喜" 字	C. yīyuàn 医 院	( )
(5)	A. zuótiān zhōngwǔ 昨 天 中 午	B. jīntiān zhōngwǔ 今 天 中 午	C. jīntiān xiàwǔ 今 天 下 午	( )

口语练习 Speaking Drills

5 听后重复。 06-8

Listen and repeat.

(1) ____________

(2) ____________

(3) ____________

(4) ____________

(5) ____________

6 听后回答。 06-9

Listen and answer.

(1) ____________

(2) ____________

(3) ____________

(4) ____________

(5) ____________

7 回答问题。

Answer the question.

Jiéhé suǒ xué nèiróng, shuōshuo nǐ xǐhuan de shuǐguǒ.
结合所 学 内容， 说说 你喜欢的 水果。

Talk about the fruits you like by integrating what you have learning in this lesson.

____

____

7 Lesson Seven

Nǐ shénme shíhou néng lái

你什么时候能来

When can you come

热身 Warm-up

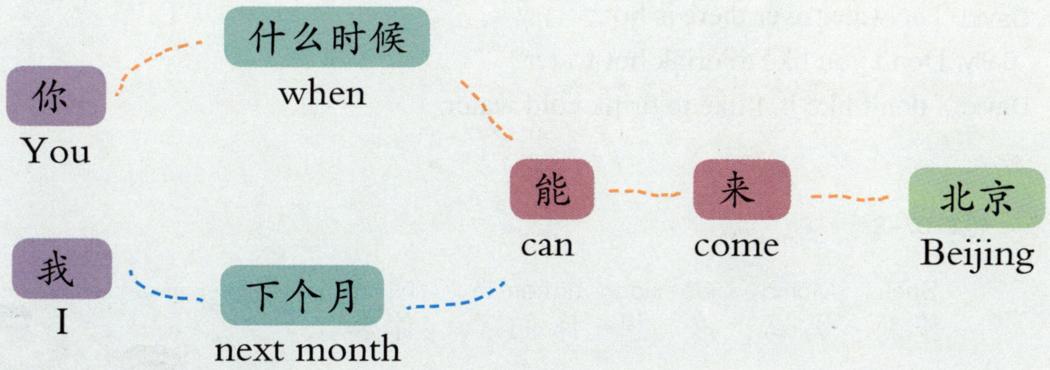

课文 Text

课文 1 07-1

Dàwèi: Zhèr de shuǐ néng hē ma?
大卫：这儿的水能喝吗？

Shālì: Zhèr de shuǐ bù néng hē.
莎莉：这儿的水不能喝。

Nàr de shuǐ néng hē.
那儿的水能喝。

Dàwèi: Nàr de shuǐ hěn rè.
大卫：那儿的水很热。

Shālì: Nǐ bù xǐhuan hē rè shuǐ ma?
莎莉：你不喜欢喝热水吗？

Dàwèi: Wǒ bù xǐhuan. Wǒ xǐhuan hē lěng shuǐ.
大卫：我不喜欢。我喜欢喝冷水。

Text One

David: Can I drink the water here?
Sally: You can't drink the water here. You can drink the water over there.
David: The water over there is hot.
Sally: Don't you like to drink hot water?
David: I don't like it. I like to drink cold water.

课文 2 07-2

Shālì: Māma, wǒ xiǎng nǐmen le. Nǐ hé bàba shénme shíhou néng lái Běijīng?
莎莉：妈妈，我想你们了。你和爸爸什么时候能来北京？

Shālì māma: Nǐ bàba jīnnián bù néng qù. Wǒ xià gè yuè néng qù.
莎莉妈妈：你爸爸今年不能去。我下个月能去。

Shālì: Māma, nǐ néng zài Běijīng zhù jǐ tiān?
莎莉：妈妈，你能在北京住几天？

Shālì māma: Wǒ néng zhù yí gè xīngqī.
莎莉妈妈：我能住一个星期。

Text Two

Sally: Mom, I've missed you. When can you and dad come to Beijing?

Sally's mom: Your dad can't go this year. I can go next month.

Sally: Mom, how many days can you stay in Beijing for?

Sally's mom: I can stay for one week.

课文 3 07–3

Shālì lái Běijīng yí gè yuè le. Tā hěn
莎莉来北京一个月了。她很

xiǎng bàba hé māma, tā māma xià gè yuè lái
想爸爸和妈妈，她妈妈下个月来

Běijīng, néng zài Běijīng zhù yí gè xīngqī.
北京，能在北京住一个星期。

Text Three

Sally has been in Beijing for one month. She misses her dad and mom very much; her mom will come to Beijing next month and can stay in Beijing for one week.

生词 New Words

这儿	zhèr	pron.	here
水	shuǐ	n.	water
能	néng	v.	can, be able to
喝	hē	v.	to drink
热	rè	adj.	hot
喜欢	xǐhuan	v.	to like
冷	lěng	adj.	cold
和	hé	conj.	and
时候	shíhou	n.	time

续表

来	lái	v.	to come
下	xià	n.	next
住	zhù	v.	to stay
天	tiān	m.	day
星期	xīngqī	n.	week

专有名词 Proper Nouns

北京	Běijīng	Beijing

语法点 Language Points

1 能愿动词"能"：用在动词前，表示有一种能力或可能性。例如：

The modal verb "能" : used in front of the verb to express a type of ability or possibility. For example:

这儿的水不能喝。

You can't drink the water here.

我妈妈能来北京一个星期。

My mom can come to Beijing for one week.

你能来北京吗？

Can you come to Beijing?

2 心理动词"想"：此处意思是"想念"，可以用程度副词修饰。例如：

The psychological verb "想" : here it means "to miss". It can be modified by adverbs of degree. For example:

我想家了。

I miss home.

我很想爸爸妈妈。

I miss my mom and dad very much.

3 介词"在"：后面加表示位置的词语组成介词短语，修饰后面的谓语，表示动作行为发生的位置。例如：

The preposition “在” : It forms a prepositional phrase when followed by words indicating a place or position. The prepositional phrase modifies the predicate, to indicate the place or position the action or behavior takes place at. For example:

我在北京学习中文。

[I in Beijing study Chinese] I study Chinese in Beijing.

我在商店买水果。

[I at shop buy fruit] I buy fruit at the shop.

我在饭馆吃饭。

[I at restaurant eat] I eat at the restaurant.

4 量词“个”：使用范围最广的个体量词。在表示一个完整个体的意思时，可以用“个”。例如：

The measure word “个” : the most wide-ranging individual measure word. We can use “个” when referring to a complete or whole individual unit. For example:

一个人、一个朋友、一个苹果、一个字

One person, one friend, one apple, one character

如果是一个完整的时间段，一般也可以用“个”。例如：

We generally also use “个” to refer to a whole period of time. For example:

一年有十二个月。

There are twelve months in one year.

一个月有四个星期。

There are four weeks in one month.

注意：“年”和“分钟”不能用“个”。

Note: “年” and “分钟” cannot be used with “个”.

5 时量补语：用在动词后，表示动作持续时间的长短。例如：

Time complements: used after the verb to indicate the duration of time the action lasts. For example:

我妈妈能在北京住一个星期。

My mom can stay in Beijing for one week.

我在北京住了三天。

I stayed in Beijing for three days.

练习 Drills

听力练习 Listening Drills

1 听词语，判断图片是否正确。 07–4
Listen to the words and determine whether the pictures are correct.

(1) ____

(2) ____

(3) ____

(4) ____

(5) ____

2 听句子，选择正确图片。 07–5
Listen to the sentences and choose the correct pictures.

(1)

A

B

C

(2)

A

B

C

(3)

A

B

C

（4）

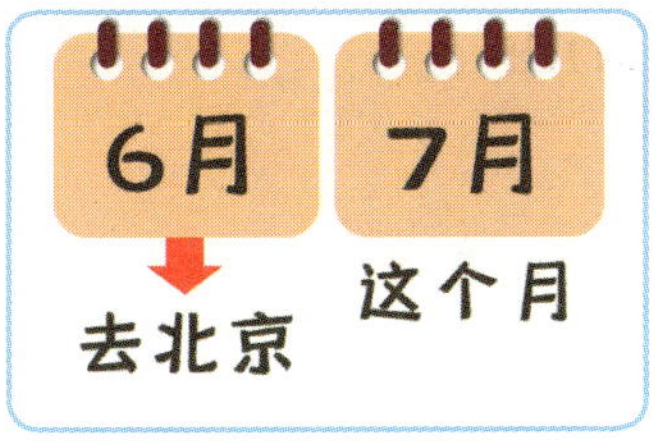

A

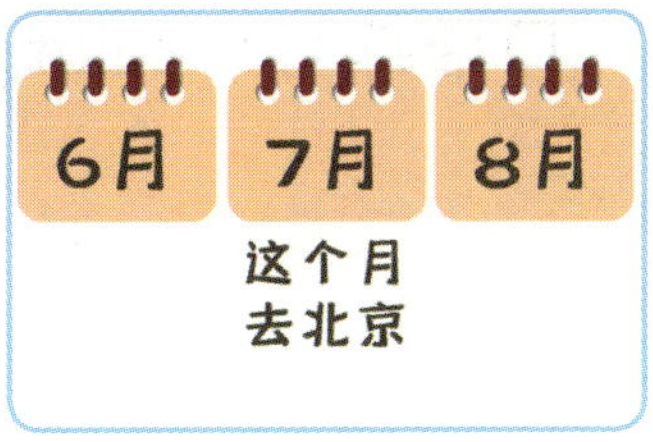

B

C

（5）

A

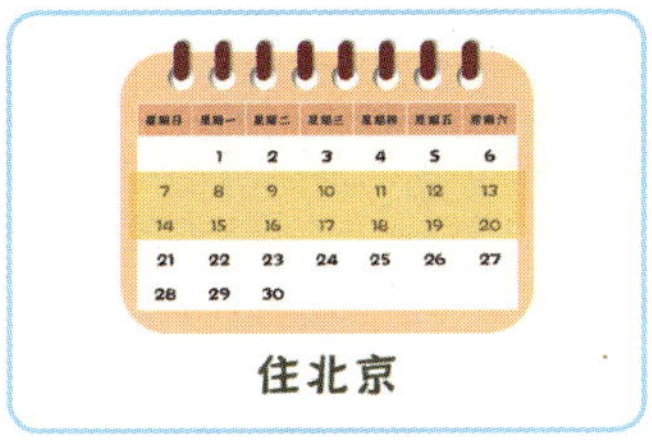

B

C

3 听对话，选择正确图片。 07–6

Listen to the conversations and choose the correct pictures.

A

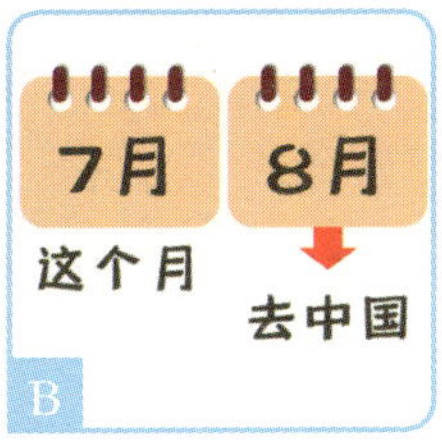

B

C

D

E

（1）		（2）	
（3）		（4）	
（5）			

4 听录音，选择正确答案。 07–7

Listen to the recordings and choose the correct answers.

（1）	A. bù néng hē 不 能 喝	B. néng hē 能 喝	C. bù xiǎng hē 不 想 喝	（　）
（2）	A. bú rè 不热	B. bù lěng 不冷	C. hěn rè 很 热	（　）
（3）	A. tā xiǎng māma 她 想 妈妈	B. tā xiǎng bàba 她 想 爸爸	C. tā xiǎng huí jiā 她 想 回 家	（　）
（4）	A. xià gè xīngqī 下 个 星期	B. xiàwǔ 下午	C. xià gè yuè 下 个 月	（　）
（5）	A. yí gè xīngqī 一个 星期	B. yì tiān 一天	C. yí gè yuè 一个 月	（　）

口语练习 Speaking Drills

5 听后重复。 07–8
Listen and repeat.

(1) ____________________

(2) ____________________

(3) ____________________

(4) ____________________

(5) ____________________

6 听后回答。 07–9
Listen and answer.

(1) ____________________

(2) ____________________

(3) ____________________

(4) ____________________

(5) ____________________

7 选词填空，读一读。
Fill in the blanks with the words and then read the text.

A. 来 (lái) B. 和 (hé) C. 想 (xiǎng) D. 月 (yuè) E. 个 (gè)

Shālì ( ) Běijīng yí gè ( ) le. Tā hěn ( ) bàba ( ) māma, tā māma xià ( ) yuè lái Běijīng, néng zài Běijīng zhù yí ( ) xīngqī.
莎莉（　）北京一个（　）了。她很（　）爸爸（　）妈妈，她妈妈下（　）月来北京，能在北京住一（　）星期。

8 Lesson Eight

Nǐ zuò jǐ diǎn de fēijī

你坐几点的飞机

What time is your flight

热身 Warm-up

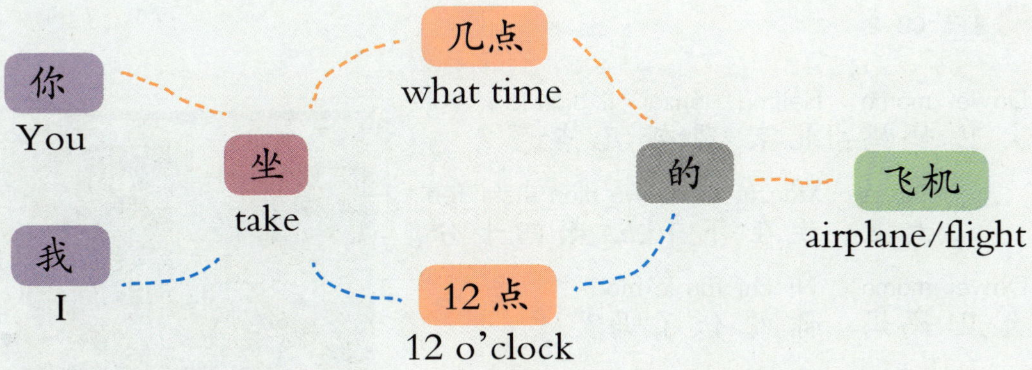

课文 Text

课文 1 08-1

Shālì: Māma, nǐ nǎ tiān lái Běijīng?
莎莉：妈妈，你哪天来北京？

Shālì māma: Wǒ shí yuè yī hào qù.
莎莉妈妈：我十月一号去。

Shālì: Nǐ zuò jǐ diǎn de fēijī?
莎莉：你坐几点的飞机？

Shālì māma: Wǒ zuò shàngwǔ bā diǎn de fēijī.
莎莉妈妈：我坐上午八点的飞机。

Text One

Sally: Mom, which day are you coming to Beijing?

Sally's mom: I'm going on October 1st.

Sally: What time is your flight?

Sally's mom: It's at eight o'clock in the morning.

课文 2 08-2

Dàwèi māma: Běijīng xiànzài jǐ diǎn le?
大卫妈妈：北京现在几点了？

Dàwèi: Xiànzài xiàwǔ wǔ diǎn sìshí fēn.
大卫：现在下午五点四十分。

Dàwèi māma: Nǐ chī fàn le ma?
大卫妈妈：你吃饭了吗？

Dàwèi: Méi chī ne, wǒ liù diǎn chī fàn.
大卫：没吃呢，我六点吃饭。

Text Two

David's mom: What time is it in Beijing now?

David: It's five forty in the afternoon now.

David's mom: Did you have dinner (meal)?

David: Not yet, I will eat at six o'clock.

课文 3 08–3

Shālì jīntiān hěn gāoxìng. Tā māma zuò
莎莉今天很高兴。她妈妈坐
shí yuè yī hào shàngwǔ bā diǎn de fēijī lái
十月一号上午八点的飞机来
Běijīng. Wǒ bàba māma shénme shíhou néng
北京。我爸爸妈妈什么时候能
lái Běijīng ne?
来北京呢？

Text Three

Sally is very happy today. Her mom will take a flight on October 1st at eight in the morning to come to Beijing. I wonder when can my dad and mom come to Beijing?

生词 New Words

哪	nǎ	pron.	which (*question*)
号	hào	n./m.	number
坐	zuò	v.	to take (a means of transportation)
飞机	fēijī	n.	airplane
八	bā	num.	eight
五	wǔ	num.	five
四十	sìshí	num.	forty
分	fēn	m.	minute
饭	fàn	n.	food
没	méi	adv.	no (*negation*)
六	liù	num.	six
点	diǎn	m.	o'clock
高兴	gāoxìng	adj.	happy

语法点 Language Points

1 疑问代词“哪”：可以用在“年、月、天”前询问日期。例如：

The interrogative pronoun “哪” : can be used in front of “年” “月” or “天” to inquire the date. For example:

你哪天去北京？

Which day are you going to Beijing?

你哪天回家？

Which day are you coming home?

“哪”常与量词连用。例如：

“哪” is often used together with measure words. For example:

你喜欢哪个杯子？

Which cup do you like?

你喜欢哪个饭馆？

Which restaurant do you like?

2 量词“号”：表示次序，多放在数字后，可以特指一个月里的日子，书面语一般用“日”。例如：

The measure word “号” : used to indicate an order or sequence. It’s usually placed after a number and can indicate a specific day within a month. In written language, “日” is used instead. For example:

昨天是九月三十日（号）。

Yesterday was September 30th.

今天是十月一日（号）。

Today is October 1st.

明天是十月二日（号）。

Tomorrow will be October 2nd.

3 时间的表达方式：中文用“点”表示整点，不是整点的时候用“分”。“点”是一昼夜的二十四分之一，“分”是一小时的六十分之一。中文的时间按从大到小的顺序，时间词放在动词前面。例如：

Ways of expressing time: “点” is used in Chinese to express a time that is on the hour, when there are no minutes (o’clock); for a time that is not on the hour we use “分”. “点”

represents one unit of the 24-hour-system and "分" represents one unit of the 60-minutes-hour. The order of time in Chinese is from big to small and nouns that express time are placed in front of the verb. For example:

我六点吃饭。

I eat dinner at six.

我十点四十五分睡觉。

I go to sleep at ten forty-five (minutes).

我坐 12 点 20 分的飞机。

I take the 12:20 plane.

4 语气助词"呢"：主要作用是缓和语气。例如：

The modal particle "呢" : mainly used to soften the tone of speech. For example:

A: 你在哪儿?

A:Where are you?

B: 我在家呢。

B: I'm at home.

A: 你吃饭了吗?

A: Have you eaten?

B: 我没吃呢。

B: Not yet.

你什么时候能来北京呢?

When can you come to Beijing?

5 日期的表达方式：中文按从大到小的顺序表达日期，先说"月"，再说"日（号）"，最后说"星期"。例如：

Ways of expressing dates: the order of a date in Chinese is from big to small. We say the month first (月), then the day (日), and lastly the weekday (星期).

昨天是九月三十日（号），星期一。

Yesterday was September 30th, Monday.

今天是十月一日（号），星期二。

Today is October 1st, Tuesday.

明天是十月二日（号），星期三。

Tomorrow will be October 2nd, Wednesday.

练习 Drills

听力练习 Listening Drills

1 听词语，判断图片是否正确。 08–4

Listen to the words and determine whether the pictures are correct.

____ ____ ____ ____ ____

2 听句子，选择正确图片。 08–5

Listen to the sentences and choose the correct pictures.

（1）

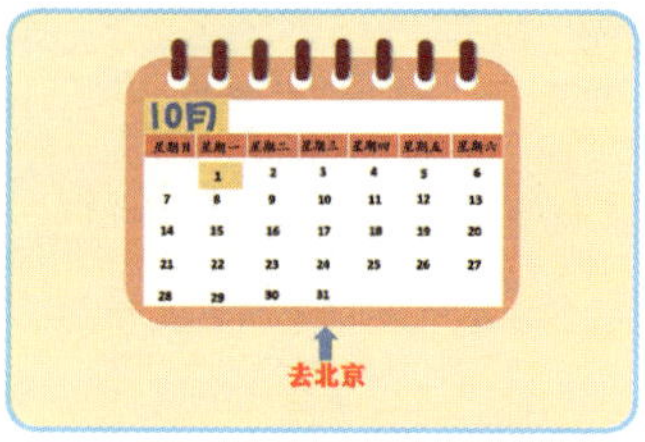

A

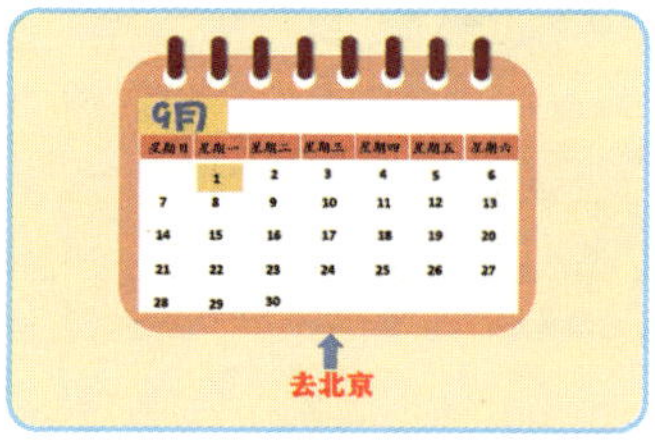

B

C

（2）

A

B

C

（3）

A

B

C

（4）

A

B

C

（5）

A

B

C

3 听对话，选择正确图片。 08-6

Listen to the conversations and choose the correct pictures.

（1）		（2）	
（3）		（4）	
（5）			

4 听录音，选择正确答案。 08-7

Listen to the recordings and choose the correct answers.

（1）A. shàngwǔ jiǔ diǎn 上午九点　B. xiàwǔ sān diǎn 下午三点　C. xiàwǔ wǔ diǎn 下午五点　（　）

（2）A. bā diǎn 八点　B. qī diǎn 七点　C. liù diǎn 六点　（　）

（3）A. fànguǎn 饭馆　B. xuéxiào 学校　C. Běijīng 北京　（　）

（4）A. zhōngwǔ shíèr diǎn 中午十二点　B. shàngwǔ shí diǎn 上午十点　C. xiàwǔ sì diǎn 下午四点　（　）

（5）A. míngtiān 明天　B. zuótiān 昨天　C. jīntiān 今天　（　）

口语练习 Speaking Drills

5 听后重复。 08-8
Listen and repeat.

（1）______

（2）______

（3）______

（4）______

（5）______

6 听后回答。 08-9
Listen and answer.

（1）______

（2）______

（3）______

（4）______

（5）______

7 选词填空，读一读。
Fill in the blanks with the words and then read the text.

A. 是 (shì)　B. 点 (diǎn)　C. 去 (qù)　D. 买 (mǎi)　E. 坐 (zuò)

Xiànzài　zhōngwǔ shíyī diǎn, wǒ shí'èr　chīfàn, xiàwǔ yī diǎn　shāngdiàn
现在（　）中午十一点，我十二（　）吃饭，下午一点（　）商店（　）

shuǐguǒ, wǔ diǎn　fēijī　Běijīng.
水果，五点（　）飞机（　）北京。

9 Lesson Nine

Nǐ zěnme le

你怎么了

What's wrong with you

热身 Warm-up

回去 Go back — 多 more — 喝 drink — 热水 hot water

回去 Go back — 多 more — 吃 eat — 水果 fruit

课文 Text

课文 1 09-1

Dàwèi: Nǐ hǎo. Nǐ shì jǐ hào?
大卫：你好。你是几号？

Níkè: Nǐ hǎo. Wǒ shì èrshísì hào. Nǐ ne?
尼克：你好。我是二十四号。你呢？

Dàwèi: Wǒ shì èrshíwǔ hào. Wǒ zài nǐ hòumiàn, nǐ zài wǒ qiánmiàn. Nǐ qiánmiàn yǒu jǐ gè rén?
大卫：我是二十五号。我在你后面，你在我前面。你前面有几个人？

Níkè: Yǒu sān gè rén.
尼克：有三个人。

Text One

David: Hi. What number are you?

Nick: Hi, I am number 24. How about you?

David: I am number 25. I'm after you, and you're before me. How many people are there before you?

Nick: There are three people.

课文 2 09-2

yīshēng: Nǐ zěnme le?
医生：你怎么了？

Dàwèi: Wǒ shuìjiào bù hǎo.
大卫：我睡觉不好。

yīshēng: Duōshao tiān le?
医生：多少天了？

Dàwèi: Sì-wǔ tiān le.
大卫：四五天了。

yīshēng: méi guānxi. Huíqù duō hē rè shuǐ, shǎo hē lěng shuǐ, duō chī shuǐguǒ.
医生：没关系。回去多喝热水，少喝冷水，多吃水果。

Text Two

Doctor: What's wrong with you?

David: I am not sleeping well.

Doctor: For how many days now?

David: About four to five days.

Doctor: That's OK. Go back and drink plenty of hot water, don't drink cold water, and eat plenty of fruit.

课文 3 09–3

Jīntiān shàngwǔ wǒ qùle yīyuàn. Zài yīyuàn wǒ rènshi le yí gè péngyou. Tā de míngzi jiào Níkè, zài Zhōngguó gōngzuò wǔ nián le. Tā de Zhōngwén hěn hǎo. Tā yǒu yí gè érzi, yí gè nǚ'ér.

今天上午我去了医院。在医院我认识了一个朋友。他的名字叫尼克，在中国工作五年了。他的中文很好。他有一个儿子，一个女儿。

Text Three

This morning I went to the hospital. I made a friend at the hospital. His name is Nick, and he's been working in China for five years. His Chinese is very good. He has a son and a daughter.

生词 New Words

前面	qiánmiàn	n.	in front (*used after the noun*)
睡觉	shuìjiào	v.	to sleep
回	huí	v.	to go back
少	shǎo	adj.	little, few
认识	rènshi	v.	to meet

续表

他	tā	pron.	he, him
工作	gōngzuò	v.	to work
年	nián	n.	year
儿子	érzi	n.	son

专有名词 Proper Nouns

尼克	Níkè	Nick
中国	Zhōngguó	China

语法点 Language Points

1 量词“号”：表示排列的次序，多放在数字后。例如：

The measure word “号” : indicates the order in which something is arranged. It’s mainly used after a number. For example:

我是 25 号。

I am number 25.

2 方位词“前面”：表示位置或次序靠前的部分。例如：

The noun of locality “前面” : indicates a position or order which is in the front. For example:

你在我前面。（次序）

You are in front of me. (order)

饭馆在商店前面。（位置）

The restaurant is in front of the store. (position)

我家在那个商店前面。（位置）

My house is in front of that store. (position)

3 “你怎么了”：表示询问。医生看病的时候常说的第一句话是“怎么了？”，意思是“有什么不舒服的地方？”。

“你怎么了” : used for inquiry. The first thing doctors usually say when seeing a patient is “怎么了”, which really means “What’s bothering you?”.

4 副词“多”：修饰动词，“多 + 动词”。例如：

The adverb “多” : modifies the verb in the construction “多+verb”. For example:

多喝热水，多吃水果。

Drink plenty of hot water and eat plenty of fruit.

不能多看电视。

You mustn't watch TV for too long.

多读书。

Read more.

练习 Drills

听力练习 Listening Drills

1 听词语，判断图片是否正确。 09–4

Listen to the words and determine whether the pictures are correct.

（1）

（2）

（3）

（4）

（5）

____　____　____　____　____

2 听句子，选择正确图片。 09–5

Listen to the sentences and choose the correct pictures.

（1）

A

B

C

(2)

A B C

(3)

A B C

(4)

A B C

(5)

A B C

3 听对话，选择正确图片。 09-6
Listen to the conversations and choose the correct pictures.

(1)		(2)	
(3)		(4)	
(5)			

4 听录音，选择正确答案。 09–7
Listen to the recordings and choose the correct answers.

	A	B	C	
(1)	A. lǎoshī jiā 老师家	B. yīyuàn 医院	C. xuéxiào 学校	( )
(2)	A. Níkè 尼克	B. péngyou 朋友	C. tóngxué 同学	( )
(3)	A. sān nián 三年	B. sì nián 四年	C. wǔ nián 五年	( )
(4)	A. bù hǎo 不好	B. hěn hǎo 很好	C. hěn rè 很热	( )
(5)	A. yí gè 一个	B. sān gè 三个	C. sì gè 四个	( )

口语练习 Speaking Drills

5 听后重复。 09–8
Listen and repeat.

(1) ______________________

(2) ______________________

(3) ______________________

(4) ______________________

(5) ______________________

6 听后回答。 09–9
Listen and answer.

(1) ______________________

(2) ______________________

(3) ______________________

(4) ______________________

(5) ______________________

7 选词填空，读一读。

Fill in the blanks with the words and then read the text.

yí gè　　shàngwǔ　　zài　　gōngzuò　　jiào　　yǒu

A. 一个　B. 上午　C. 在　D. 工作　E. 叫　F. 有

Jīntiān ( ) wǒ qùle yīyuàn. ( ) yīyuàn wǒ rènshile ( ) péngyou. Tā de míngzi ( ) Níkè, zài Zhōngguó ( ) wǔ nián le. Tā de Zhōngwén hěn hǎo. Tā ( ) yí gè érzi, yí gè nǚ'ér.

今天（　）我去了医院。（　）医院我认识了（　）朋友。他的名字（　）尼克，在中国（　）五年了。他的中文很好。他（　）一个儿子，一个女儿。

10 Lesson Ten

Xīngqītiān lái wǒ jiā chī fàn

星期天来我家吃饭

Come by my house for lunch on Sunday

热身 Warm-up

我们 (We) — 买 (buy) — 了 — 一些 (some) — 有字的 (with characters) — 苹果 (apple)

我们 (We) — 吃 (eat) — 了 — 很多 (many) — 好吃的 (delicious) — 东西 (thing)

课文 Text

课文 1 10–1

Níkè: Xīngqītiān lái wǒ jiā chī fàn, zěnmeyàng?
尼克：星期天来我家吃饭，怎么样？
Nǐ hé nǐ de péngyou dōu lái.
你和你的朋友都来。

Dàwèi: Tài hǎo le. Xièxie. Nǐ jiā zài nǎr?
大卫：太好了。谢谢。你家在哪儿？

Níkè: Bú kèqi. Wǒ jiā zài nǐmen xuéxiào qiánmiàn, nǐ kàn, zhè shì xuéxiào, zhè shì wǒ jiā.
尼克：不客气。我家在你们学校前面，你看，这是学校，这是我家。

Dàwèi: Wǒmen jǐ diǎn qù?
大卫：我们几点去？

Níkè: Shàngwǔ shí diǎn zěnmeyàng?
尼克：上午十点怎么样？

Dàwèi: Hěn hǎo. Xièxie nǐ.
大卫：很好。谢谢你。

Text One

Nick: Come by my house for lunch on Sunday, how about it? Come together with your friend.
David: That's great, thank you. Where do you live?
Nick: You're welcome. My house is in front of your school. Look (looking at a map on the phone), this is the school here and this is my house.
David: What time should we go?
Nick: How about ten in the morning?
David: Very well. Thank you.

课文 2 10–2

Shālì: Míngtiān qù Níkè jiā, wǒmen mǎi xiē shénme?
莎莉：明天去尼克家，我们买些什么？

Dàwèi: Chá hé shuǐguǒ zěnmeyàng?
大卫：茶和水果怎么样？

Shālì : Chá hé shuǐguǒ dōu hěn hǎo.
莎莉：茶 和 水果 都 很 好。

Dàwèi : Chá wǒ zhèr yǒu yìxiē.
大卫：茶 我 这儿 有 一些。

Shālì : Tài hǎo le. Wǒ qù mǎi yìxiē shuǐguǒ.
莎莉：太 好 了。我 去 买 一些 水果。

Text Two

Sally: We're going to Nick's house tomorrow. What should we buy?
David: How about tea and fruit?
Sally: Tea and fruit are both very good.
David: I have some tea (at home).
Sally: That's great. I'll go buy some fruit.

课文 3 10–3

Zuótiān xià yǔ le, wǒ hé Shālì qùle
昨天 下 雨 了，我 和 莎莉 去 了
Níkè jiā. Wǒmen mǎile yìxiē yǒu zì de
尼克家。我们 买了 一些 有 字 的
píngguǒ. Zài Níkè jiā, wǒmen chīle hěn
苹果。在 尼克家，我们 吃了 很
duō hǎochī de dōngxi, hēle hěn hǎohē de
多 好吃 的 东西，喝了 很 好喝 的
Zhōngguó chá.
中国 茶。

Text Three

Yesterday it rained, Sally and I went to Nick's house. We bought some apples with characters on them. At Nick's house, we ate a lot of delicious things and drank a lot of tasty tea.

生词 New Words

星期天	xīngqītiān	n.	Sunday
怎么样	zěnmeyàng	pron.	how about it? what do you think?

续表

都	dōu	adv.	both, all
太	tài	adv.	too
不客气	bú kèqi		you're welcome; don't mention it
十	shí	num.	ten
茶	chá	n.	tea
下雨	xià yǔ		to rain
东西	dōngxi	n.	thing, object

语法点 Language Points

1 疑问代词"怎么样"：在本课中用来询问别人的意见。例如：

The interrogative pronoun "怎么样" : in this lesson it is used to inquire other people's opinion. For example:

星期天来我家吃饭，怎么样？

Come by my house for lunch on Sunday, how about it?

上午十点怎么样？

How about ten in the morning?

2 副词"都"：表示全部。"都"的位置一般放在动词或形容词前，总括的对象后。例如：

The adverb "都" : used to express totality. "都" is usually placed after the object that's being summed up, but before the verb or the adjective. For example:

茶和水果都很好。

[Tea and fruit both very good] Tea and fruit are both very good.

昨天和今天都下雨了。

[Yesterday and today both rained] It rained both yesterday and today.

3 "太……了"：感叹句，表示感叹、惊讶。例如：

"太……了": the construction forms an exclamatory sentence, used to express exclamation or surprise. For example:

太好了！

[Too good] That's great!

这水太热了！

[This water too hot] The water is too hot!

今天太冷了！

[Today too cold] It's extremely cold today!

4 “不客气”：礼貌用语，用于回答别人的感谢，相当于“不用谢”。

“不客气”: polite expression, used as a reply to people's thanks, equivalent to “no need to thank me”.

5 “好”+感官动词：“好吃”用于食物，“好喝”用于饮品。中文用“好”+感官动词表示好的感觉，可以用程度副词修饰。例如：

“好”+ sense verb : “好吃” is used to describe foods and “好喝” to describe drinks. In Chinese, the construction “好”+ sense verb is used to express a type of positive sensation. It can be modified by a degree adverb. For example:

这个苹果很好吃。

This apple is delicious.

中国菜很好吃。

Chinese food is delicious.

中国茶很好喝。

Chinese tea is delicious.

练习 Drills

听力练习 Listening Drills

1 听词语，判断图片是否正确。 10-4

Listen to the words and determine whether the pictures are correct.

(1) ______

(2) ______

(3) ______

(4) ______

(5) ______

2 听句子，选择正确图片。 10-5
Listen to the sentences and choose the correct pictures.

(1)

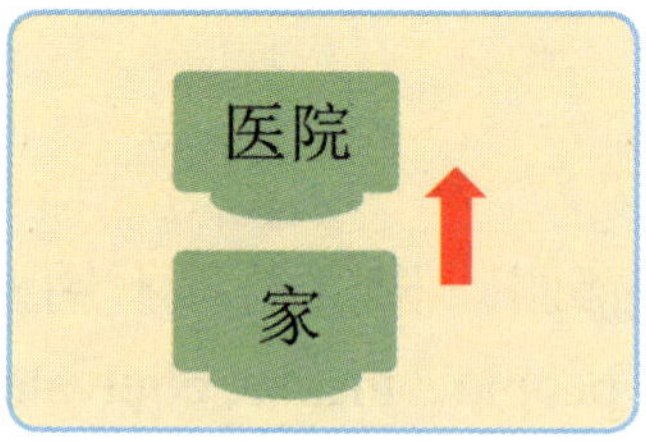

A

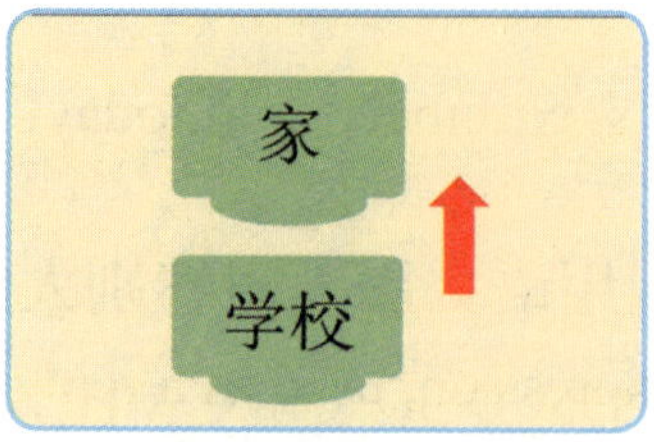

B

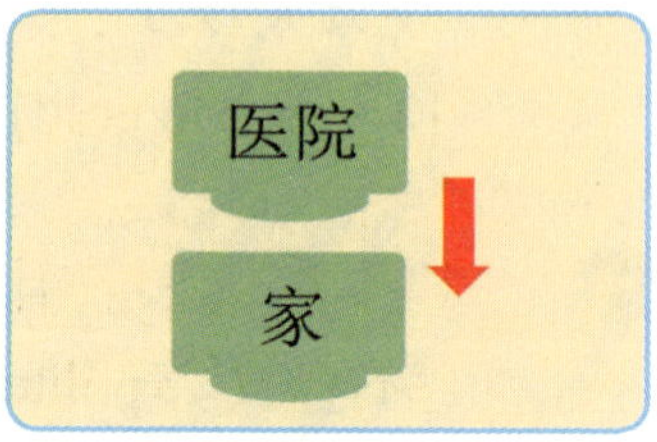

C

(2)

A

B

C

(3)

A

B

C

(4)

A

B

C

(5)

A

B

C

3 听对话，选择正确图片。 10–6

Listen to the conversations and choose the correct pictures.

(1)		(2)	
(3)		(4)	
(5)			

4 听录音，选择正确答案。 10–7

Listen to the recordings and choose the correct answers.

	A	B	C	
(1)	A. qù xuéxiào 去学校	B. Níkè jiā 尼克家	C. qù huǒchēzhàn 去火车站	( )
(2)	A. zài xuéxiào li 在学校里	B. zài xuéxiào qiánmiàn 在学校前面	C. zài Běijīng 在北京	( )
(3)	A. shàngwǔ bā diǎn 上午八点	B. zhōngwǔ shíèr diǎn 中午十二点	C. shàngwǔ shí diǎn 上午十点	( )
(4)	A. yǒu zì de píngguǒ 有字的苹果	B. yīfu 衣服	C. yǐzi 椅子	( )
(5)	A. hǎochī de dōngxi 好吃的东西	B. píngguǒ 苹果	C. mǐfàn 米饭	( )

口语练习 Speaking Drills

5 听后重复。 10–8

Listen and repeat.

(1) ____________________

(2) ____________________

(3) ____________________

(4) ____________________

(5) ____________________

6 听后回答。 10-9
Listen and answer.

(1) ______________________________

(2) ______________________________

(3) ______________________________

(4) ______________________________

(5) ______________________________

7 选词填空，读一读。
Fill in the blanks with the words and then read the text.

hǎochī　　le　　zài　　xiē　　hǎohē
A. 好吃　B. 了　C. 在　D. 些　E. 好喝

Zuótiān, wǒ qù　　Níkè jiā. Wǒmen mǎi　　yì　　yǒu zì de píngguǒ.
昨天，我去（　）尼克家。我们买（　）一（　）有字的苹果。（　）

Níkè jiā, wǒmen chī　　hěn duō　　de dōngxi, hēle hěn　　de Zhōngguó chá.
尼克家，我们吃（　）很多（　）的东西，喝了很（　）的中国茶。

11 Lesson Eleven

Wǒ zài kàn diànyǐng ne

我在看电影呢

I am watching a movie

热身 Warm-up

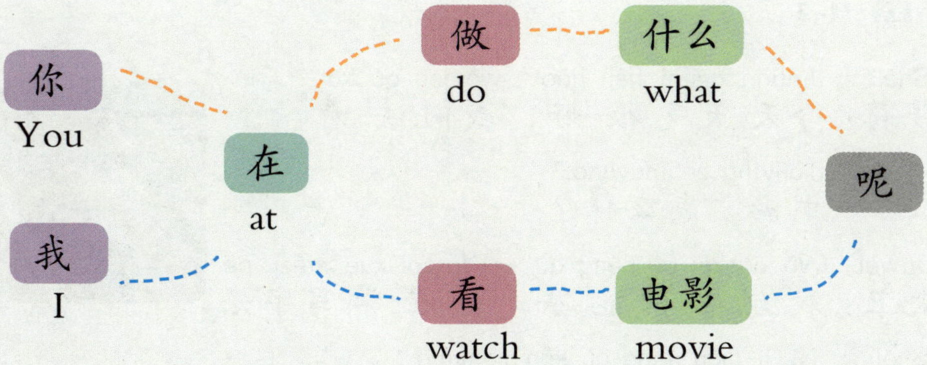

课文 Text

课文 1 11-1

Shālì : Wèi, wǒ shì Shālì. Nǐ zài zuò shénme ne?
莎莉：喂，我是莎莉。你在做什么呢？

Dàwèi : Wǒ zài kàn diànyǐng ne. Nǐ ne?
大卫：我在看电影呢。你呢？

Shālì : Wǒ zài mǎi yīfu ne. Nǐ zài kàn shénme diànyǐng?
莎莉：我在买衣服呢。你在看什么电影？

Dàwèi : Wǒ zài kàn yí gè Zhōngguó diànyǐng.
大卫：我在看一个中国电影。

Text One

Sally: Hello, this is Sally. What are you doing?
David: I am watching a movie. And you?
Sally: I am buying clothes. What movie are you watching?
David: I am watching a Chinese movie.

课文 2 11-2

Shālì : Jīntiān tiānqì hěn hǎo, wǒmen qù kàn diànyǐng zěnmeyàng?
莎莉：今天天气很好，我们去看电影怎么样？

Dàwèi : Wǒ xiànzài bù néng qù. Wǒ zài xué xiězì ne.
大卫：我现在不能去。我在学写字呢。

Shālì : Nǐ jǐ diǎn néng qù kàn diànyǐng?
莎莉：你几点能去看电影？

Dàwèi : Wǒ wǔ diǎn néng qù.
大卫：我五点能去。

Text Two

Sally: The weather today is great, so how about go to see a movie?
David: I can't go now. I am learning to write characters.
Sally: What time can you go to see a movie?
David: I can go at five o'clock.

课文 3 11–3

Jīntiān xīngqī liù, Shālì dǎle liǎng gè
今天 星期 六，莎莉打了 两 个

diànhuà lái. Shàngwǔ Shālì dǎ diànhuà de
电话 来。上午 莎莉打 电话 的

shíhou, wǒ zài kàn diànyǐng. Xiàwǔ tā dǎ
时候，我 在 看 电影。下午 她 打

diànhuà de shíhou, wǒ zài xué xiězì.
电话 的 时候，我 在 学 写字。

Text Three

Today is Saturday. Sally called me on the phone twice. In the morning when Sally called, I was watching a movie. In the afternoon when she called, I was learning to write characters.

生词 New Words

喂	wèi	int.	hello (on the phone)
电影	diànyǐng	n.	movie
衣服	yīfu	n.	clothes
天气	tiānqì	n.	weather
打电话	dǎ diànhuà		to call (on the phone), to make a phone call
两	liǎng	num.	two

语法点 Language Points

1 "呢"：和"在"一起构成"在……呢"，表示动作正在进行。例如：

"呢": used together with "在" to form the construction "在……呢", which expresses an action in progress at the moment of speech. For example:

A：你在做什么呢？

A：What are you doing?

B：我在看电影呢。

B：I am watching a movie.

注意："呢"可以省略，省略后不影响句子的意思，只影响句子的语气。有"呢"的句子语气比较和缓。例如：

Note: "呢" can be omitted. If omitted, the meaning of the sentence stays the same, however the tone of the sentence will change. Having "呢" gives the sentence a softer tone.

A：你在做什么？

A：What are you doing?

B：我在买衣服。

B：I am buying clothes.

2 "在"＋动词＋（宾语）＋"呢"：表示动作正在进行。例如：

"在"+ verb + (object) +"呢" : expresses an action in progress at the moment of speech. For example:

我在看书呢。

I am reading a book.

我在学写字呢。

I am learning to write characters.

我在看电影呢。

I am watching a movie.

注意：这里"在"是副词，不是"在"＋地方的"在"，也不是"在"＋地方＋谓语的"在"。例如：

Note: The "在" in "在" + verb+(object) +"呢" is an adverb, and it's different from the "在" in "在" + place or in "在" + place + predicate. For example:

（1）"在"是动词。

"在" is a verb.

A：你在哪儿？

A：Where are you?

B：我在商店。

B：I am at the shop.

（2）"在"是介词。

"在" is a preposition.

A：你在哪儿学习汉语？

A：Where do you study Chinese?

B：我在北京学习汉语。

B：I study Chinese in Beijing.

（3） "在" 是副词。

"在" is an adverb.

A：你在做什么呢？

A：What are you doing?

B：我在买衣服呢。

B：I am buying clothes.

3 动词 + "了" +（数量词）宾语：句子中有动态助词 "了"，动词后有宾语时，宾语一般要有数量词等定语。例如：

verb +"了"+ (quantifier) object : when the dynamic auxiliary "了" is present in the sentence and the verb is followed by an object, this object should be preceded by a quantifier that acts as an attributive. For example:

上午莎莉打了两个电话。

Sally called two times in the morning.

昨天我吃了两个苹果。

I ate two apples yesterday.

今天我写了九十九个字。

I wrote 99 characters today.

练习 Drills

听力练习 Listening Drills

1 听词语，判断图片是否正确。 11-4

Listen to the words and determine whether the pictures are correct.

（1）

（2）

（3）

（4）

（5）

____ ____ ____ ____ ____

2 听句子，选择正确图片。 11-5
Listen to the sentences and choose the correct pictures.

（1）

A

B

C

（2）

A

B

C

（3）

A

B

C

（4）

A

B

C

（5）

A

B

C

3 听对话，选择正确图片。 11-6

Listen to the conversations and choose the correct pictures.

(1)		(2)	
(3)		(4)	
(5)			

4 听录音，选择正确答案。 11-7

Listen to the recordings and choose the correct answers.

	A	B	C	
(1)	tiānqì bù hǎo A. 天气不好	tiānqì hěn hǎo B. 天气很 好	tiānqì hěn rè C. 天气很 热	( )
(2)	kàn diànyǐng A. 看 电 影	shuìjiào B. 睡 觉	kàn shū C. 看 书	( )
(3)	mǎi píngguǒ A. 买 苹 果	mǎi zhuōzi B. 买 桌子	mǎi yīfu C. 买 衣服	( )
(4)	xiàwǔ yī diǎn A. 下午 一点	xiàwǔ sān diǎn B. 下午 三 点	xiàwǔ wǔ diǎn C. 下午 五 点	( )
(5)	tā zài shuìjiào A. 他在 睡 觉	tā zài kàn shū B. 他在 看 书	tā zài chī fàn C. 他在 吃 饭	( )

口语练习 Speaking Drills

5 听后重复。 11-8

Listen and repeat.

(1) ____________________

(2) ____________________

(3) ____________________

(4) ____________________

(5) ____________________

6 听后回答。 11-9
Listen and answer.

(1) ______

(2) ______

(3) ______

(4) ______

(5) ______

7 选词填空，读一读。
Fill in the blanks with the words and then read the text.

hěn A. 很　lái B. 来　le C. 了　shíhou D. 时候　zài E. 在

Jīntiān xīngqī liù, tiānqì ( ) hǎo. Shālì dǎ ( ) liǎng gè diànhuà ( ). Shàngwǔ Shālì dǎ diànhuà de ( ), wǒ ( ) kàn diànyǐng. Xiàwǔ tā dǎ diànhuà de shíhou, wǒ ( ) xué xiězì.

今天星期六，天气（　）好。莎莉打（　）两个电话（　）。上午莎莉打电话的（　），我（　）看电影。下午她打电话的时候，我（　）学写字。

12 Lesson Twelve

Wǒ shì zuótiān xiàwǔ lái de
我是昨天下午来的
I came yesterday afternoon

热身
Warm-up

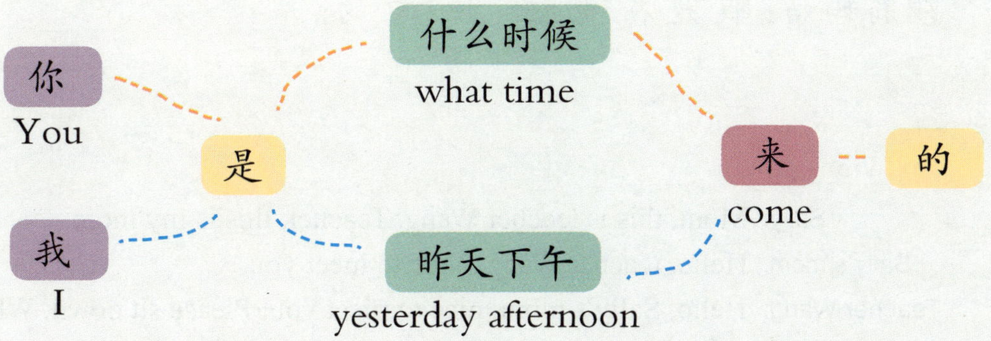

课文 Text

课文 1 12-1

Shālì: Māma, zhè shì Wáng lǎoshī.
莎莉：妈妈，这是王老师。

Lǎoshī, zhè shì wǒ māma.
老师，这是我妈妈。

Shālì māma: Nǐ hǎo, Wáng lǎoshī. Rènshi nǐ hěn gāoxìng.
莎莉妈妈：你好，王老师。认识你很高兴。

Wáng lǎoshī: Nǐ hǎo, Shālì māma. Rènshi nǐ hěn gāoxìng. Qǐng zuò. Nǐ shì shénme shíhou lái de?
王老师：你好，莎莉妈妈。认识你很高兴。请坐。你是什么时候来的？

Shālì māma: Wáng lǎoshī, wǒ shì zuótiān xiàwǔ lái de.
莎莉妈妈：王老师，我是昨天下午来的。

Wáng lǎoshī: Nǐ de Zhōngwén hěn hǎo. Nǐ shì zěnme xuéxí Zhōngwén de?
王老师：你的中文很好。你是怎么学习中文的？

Shālì māma: Wǒ shì zài diànnǎo shang xué de.
莎莉妈妈：我是在电脑上学的。

Text One

Sally: Mom, this is teacher Wang. Teacher, this is my mom.

Sally's mom: Hello, teacher Wang. Nice to meet you.

Teacher Wang: Hello, Sally's mom, nice to meet you. Please sit down. When did you come?

Sally's mom: Teacher Wang, I came yesterday afternoon.

Teacher Wang: Your Chinese is very good. How did you learn Chinese?

Sally's mom: I learned it on the computer.

课文 2 12-2

Dàwèi māma: Níkè shì shéi? Nǐmen shì zěnme rènshi de?
大卫妈妈：尼克是谁？你们是怎么认识的？

Dàwèi: Tā shì wǒ de yí gè péngyou. Wǒmen shì zài yīyuàn rènshi de.
大卫：他是我的一个朋友。我们是在医院认识的。

Dàwèi māma: Tā qù Zhōngguó jǐ nián le?
大卫妈妈：他去中国几年了？

Dàwèi: Tā láile wǔ nián le.
大卫：他来了五年了。

Text Two

David's mom: Who is Nick? How did you meet?

David: He is a friend of mine. We met at the hospital.

David's mom: When did he go to China?

David: He's been here for five years.

课文 3 12-3

Shālì de māma shì zuótiān xiàwǔ lái de. Zhè jǐ tiān Běijīng tiānqì hěn hǎo, méiyǒu xià yǔ, bùlěng-búrè, tā māma hěn xǐhuan. Tāmen yì jiā rén dōu hěn xǐhuan Zhōngguó, dōu zài xuéxí Zhōngwén.

莎莉的妈妈是昨天下午来的。这几天北京天气很好，没有下雨，不冷不热，她妈妈很喜欢。她们一家人都很喜欢中国，都在学习中文。

Text Three

Sally's mom came yesterday afternoon. The weather in Beijing these days is very nice, it's not raining and it's neither cold nor hot, and her mom likes it a lot. The both of them like China a lot, and they're both learning Chinese.

生词 New Words

请	qǐng	v.	please
学习	xuéxí	v.	to learn, to study
电脑	diànnǎo	n.	computer
谁	shéi	pron.	who
没有	méiyǒu	adv.	not, no
她们	tāmen	pron.	they, them (*female*)

语法点 Language Points

1 “是……的”：是一种强调句，强调部分放在“是……的”中间，可以强调时间、地点、方式等。例如：

“是……的” : it's a type of sentence construction used for emphasis, with the object of emphasis being placed between “是” and “的”. It can emphasize the time, the place, the manner, etc. For example:

你是什么时候来的？（强调时间）

When did you come? (emphasizes the time)

你的书是在哪儿买的？（强调地点）

Where did you buy your book? (emphasizes the place)

你是怎么来的？（强调方式）

How did you come? (emphasizes the manner)

否定句为“不是……的”。例如：

The negative form of this construction is “不是……的”. For example:

我不是昨天来的。

I didn't come yesterday.

这本书不是在那个商店买的。

I didn't buy this book at that store.

我不是坐出租车来的。

I didn't come by taxi.

2 “不……不……”：用在同类而意思相对的词或词素的前面，意思是“既不……也不……”，表示适中、恰到好处，如“不冷不热”“不大不小”“不多不少”。例如：

“不……不……”: used in front of words or morphemes belonging to the same category but with opposite meanings, meaning “neither…nor…”. It indicates that something is moderate or just right, just like “neither hot nor cold” “neither big nor small” “neither many nor few”. For example:

北京的天气不冷不热。

The weather in Beijing is neither cold nor hot.

我买的苹果不大不小。

The apples I bought are neither big nor small.

我的家不大不小。

My house is neither big nor small.

3 “认识你很高兴”：初次见面时的常用语。也可以说“很高兴认识你”。

“认识你很高兴” : common expression used when meeting someone for the first time. We can also say “很高兴认识你”.

4 “这几天”：意思是最近的几天。

“这几天” : indicates the few recent days.

5 “一家人”：意思是全家，常与人称代词复数一起构成人称代词 + “一家人” + “都” + 动词的句子。例如：

“一家人” : indicates the whole family and is often used together with personal pronouns in the plural to form the construction personal pronoun+“一家人”+“都”+verb. For example:

他们一家人都喜欢看书。

Their whole family likes to read books.

我们一家人都喜欢学中文。

Our whole family likes to learn Chinese.

你们一家人昨天去哪儿了？

Where did your whole family go yesterday?

练习 Drills

听力练习 Listening Drills

1 听词语，判断图片是否正确。 12-4
Listen to the words and determine whether the pictures are correct.

(1) ______

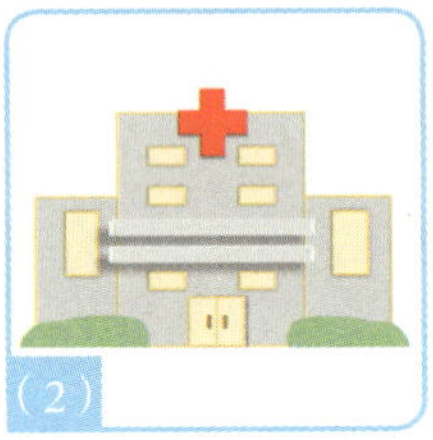
(2) ______

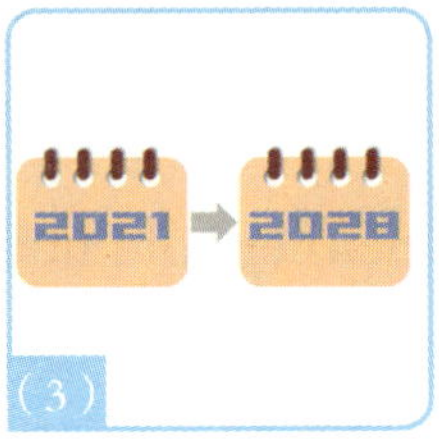

(3) ______

(4) ______

(5) ______

2 听句子，选择正确图片。 12-5
Listen to the sentences and choose the correct pictures.

(1)

A

B

C

(2)

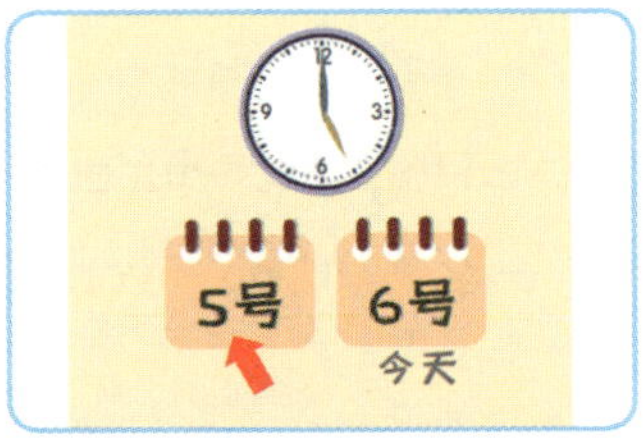

A

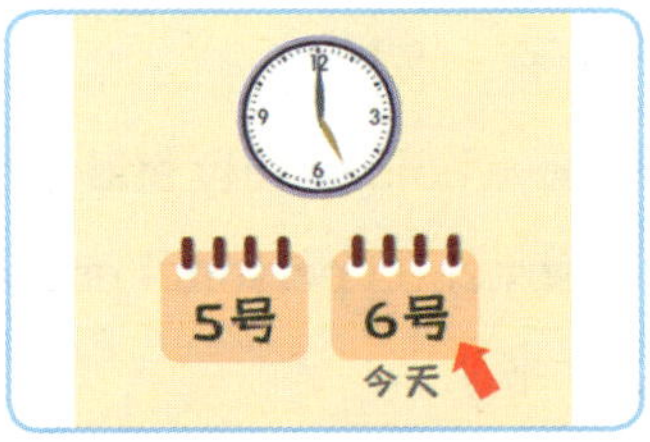

B

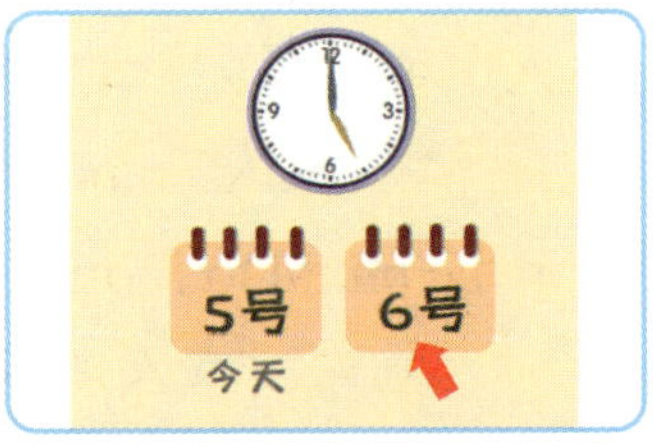

C

(3)

A

B

C

(4)

A

B

C

(5)

A

B

C

3 听对话，选择正确图片。 12–6

Listen to the conversations and choose the correct pictures.

A

B

C

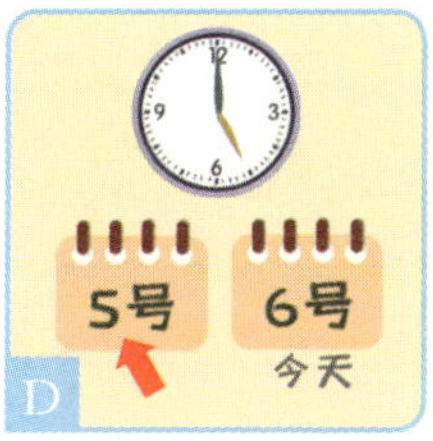

D

E

(1)		(2)	
(3)		(4)	
(5)			

4 听录音，选择正确答案。 12–7

Listen to the recordings and choose the correct answers.

(1)	A. míngtiān xiàwǔ 明天下午	B. zuótiān xiàwǔ 昨天下午	C. zuótiān shàngwǔ 昨天上午	( )
(2)	A. hěn lěng 很冷	B. bùlěng - búrè 不冷不热	C. hěn rè 很热	( )
(3)	A. hěn xǐhuan 很喜欢	B. bù xǐhuan 不喜欢	C. hěn xiǎng jiā 很想家	( )
(4)	A. xué xiě zì 学写字	B. xué zuò Zhōngguó cài 学做中国菜	C. xué Zhōngwén 学中文	( )
(5)	A. zài xuéxiào 在学校	B. zài shāngdiàn 在商店	C. zài yīyuàn 在医院	( )

口语练习 Speaking Drills

5 听后重复。 11-8
Listen and repeat.

(1) ______________________________

(2) ______________________________

(3) ______________________________

(4) ______________________________

(5) ______________________________

6 听后回答。 11-9
Listen and answer.

(1) ______________________________

(2) ______________________________

(3) ______________________________

(4) ______________________________

(5) ______________________________

7 选词填空，读一读。
Fill in the blanks with the words and then read the text.

A. 不 bù　B. 都 dōu　C. 是 shì　D. 一 yì　E. 很 hěn

Tā māma　zuótiān xiàwǔ lái de. Zhè jǐ tiān Běijīng tiānqì hěn hǎo,　lěng-bú
她 妈妈（　）昨天 下午 来的。这 几天 北京 天气 很 好，（　）冷 不

rè,　tā māma　xǐhuan. Tāmen　jiā rén　hěn xǐhuan Zhōngguó,　zài
热，她 妈妈（　）喜欢。她们（　）家人（　）很 喜欢 中国，（　）在

xuéxí Zhōngwén.
学习 中文。

词汇总表 Vocabulary

生词 New Words

词语 Word/Phrase	拼音 *Pinyin*	词性 Part of Speech	词义 Meaning	课号 Lesson
			A	
爱	ài	v.	to like, to love	4
			B	
八	bā	num.	eight	8
爸爸	bàba	n.	dad, father	1
杯子	bēizi	n.	cup, glass	4
不	bù	adv.	no, not	5
不客气	bú kèqi		you're welcome; don't mention it	10
			C	
中国菜	Zhōngguó cài	n.	Chinese food/dishes	3
茶	chá	n.	tea	10
吃	chī	v.	to eat	4
			D	
打电话	dǎ diànhuà		to call (on the phone), to make a phone call	11
大	dà	adj.	big	2
的	de	part.	*used to indicate possession*	1
点	diǎn	m.	o'clock	8
电脑	diànnǎo	n.	computer	12
电影	diànyǐng	n.	movie	11

续表

词语 Word/Phrase	拼音 *Pinyin*	词性 Part of Speech	词义 Meaning	课号 Lesson
东西	dōngxi	n.	thing, object	10
都	dōu	adv.	both, all	10
读	dú	v.	to read, to pronounce	3
对不起	duìbuqǐ	v.	I'm sorry	3
多	duō	adj.	many, much	2
多少	duōshao	pron.	how much	5
		E		
儿子	érzi	n.	son	9
二十	èrshí	num.	twenty	5
		F		
饭	fàn	n.	food	8
饭馆	fànguǎn	n.	restaurant	4
飞机	fēijī	n.	airplane	8
分	fēn	m.	minute	8
		G		
高兴	gāoxìng	adj.	happy	8
个	gè	m.	*measure word*	2
工作	gōngzuò	v.	to work	9
狗	gǒu	n.	dog	2
		H		
汉字	Hànzì	n.	Chinese character, Hanzi	3
好	hǎo	adj.	good	1
号	hào	n./m.	number	8
喝	hē	v.	to drink	7
和	hé	conj.	and	7

续表

词语 Word/Phrase	拼音 *Pinyin*	词性 Part of Speech	词义 Meaning	课号 Lesson
很	hěn	adv.	very	2
后面	hòumiàn	n.	behind (*used after the noun*)	6
回	huí	v.	to go back	9
会	huì	v.	can, to be able to	3
			J	
几	jǐ	pron.	how many	2
家	jiā	n.	family, home	2
叫	jiào	v.	to be called (a name), one's name is	1
今年	jīnnián	n.	this year	2
今天	jīntiān	n.	today	3
			K	
看	kàn	v.	to look, to see	3
块	kuài	m.	*kuai* (spoken version of *yuan*, the basic unit of money in China)	5
			L	
来	lái	v.	to come	7
老师	lǎoshī	n.	teacher	1
了	le	part.	*used at the end of or in the middle of a sentence, to indicate a change or a new circumstance*	2
冷	lěng	adj.	cold	7
里	li	n.	inside (*used after the noun*)	6
两	liǎng	num.	two	11
零	líng	num.	zero	2
六	liù	num.	six	8
			M	
妈妈	māma	n.	mom, mother	1

续表

词语 Word/Phrase	拼音 *Pinyin*	词性 Part of Speech	词义 Meaning	课号 Lesson
吗	ma	part.	*used at the end of a question*	2
买	mǎi	v.	to buy	4
没	méi	adv.	no (*negation*)	8
没关系	méi guānxi		no problem	3
没有	méiyǒu	adv.	not, no	12
米饭	mǐfàn	n.	cooked rice	4
名字	míngzi	n.	name	1
明天	míngtiān	n.	tomorrow	4
		N		
哪	nǎ	pron.	which (*question*)	8
哪儿	nǎr	pron.	where (*question*)	5
那儿	nàr	pron.	there	6
呢	ne	aux.	*used at the end of the sentence*	1
能	néng	v.	can, be able to	7
你	nǐ	pron.	you (*sg.*)	1
你们	nǐmen	pron.	you (*pl.*)	1
年	nián	n.	year	9
您	nín	pron.	you (*polite form*)	2
女儿	nǚ'ér	n.	daughter	2
		P		
朋友	péngyou	n.	friend	6
漂亮	piàoliang	adj.	pretty, beautiful	2
苹果	píngguǒ	n.	apple	2
		Q		
七十	qīshí	num.	seventy	5

续表

词语 Word/Phrase	拼音 *Pinyin*	词性 Part of Speech	词义 Meaning	课号 Lesson
前面	qiánmiàn	n.	in front (*used after the noun*)	9
钱	qián	n.	money	5
请	qǐng	v.	please	12
去	qù	v.	to go	4
		R		
热	rè	adj.	hot	7
人	rén	n.	person, people	1
认识	rènshi	v.	to meet	9
		S		
三	sān	num.	three	2
三十	sānshí	num.	thirty	2
商店	shāngdiàn	n.	store, shop	4
上	shang	n.	on (*used after the noun*)	6
上午	shàngwǔ	n.	morning	4
少	shǎo	adj.	little, few	9
什么	shénme	pron.	what	1
十	shí	num.	ten	10
时候	shíhou	n.	time	7
是	shì	v.	to be	1
谁	shéi	pron.	who	12
水	shuǐ	n.	water	7
水果	shuǐguǒ	n.	fruit	6
睡觉	shuìjiào	v.	to sleep	9
说	shuō	v.	to say	3
四十	sìshí	num.	forty	8

续表

词语 Word/Phrase	拼音 *Pinyin*	词性 Part of Speech	词义 Meaning	课号 Lesson
岁	suì	n.	years (of age)	2
			T	
他	tā	pron.	he, him	9
她	tā	pron.	she, her	1
她们	tāmen	pron.	they, them (*female*)	12
太	tài	adv.	too	10
天	tiān	m.	day	7
天气	tiānqì	n.	weather	11
同学	tóngxué	n.	classmate	1
			W	
喂	wèi	int.	hello (on the phone)	11
我	wǒ	pron.	I, me	1
我们	wǒmen	pron.	we, us	6
五	wǔ	num.	five	8
			X	
喜欢	xǐhuan	v.	to like	7
下	xià	n.	next	7
下午	xiàwǔ	n.	afternoon	4
下雨	xià yǔ		to rain	10
现在	xiànzài	n.	now	2
想	xiǎng	v./mod.	to want, to miss	4
小	xiǎo	adj.	small, little	2
些	xiē	m.	some	6
写	xiě	v.	to write	3
谢谢	xièxie	v.	thank you	5

续表

词语 Word/Phrase	拼音 *Pinyin*	词性 Part of Speech	词义 Meaning	课号 Lesson
星期	xīngqī	n.	week	7
星期六	xīngqī liù	n.	Saturday	4
星期天	xīngqītiān	n.	Sunday	10
学	xué	v.	to learn	4
学生	xuéshēng	n.	student	6
学习	xuéxí	v.	to learn, to study	12
学校	xuéxiào	n.	school	4
		Y		
一	yī	num.	one	2
衣服	yīfu	n.	clothes	11
医生	yīshēng	n.	doctor	6
医院	yīyuàn	n.	hospital	6
有	yǒu	v.	to have, to exist	5
月	yuè	n.	month	2
		Z		
在	zài	v./prep.	to be at/in/on	6
怎么	zěnme	pron.	how	3
怎么样	zěnmeyàng	pron.	how about it? what do you think?	10
这	zhè	pron.	this	2
这儿	zhèr	pron.	here	7
这么	zhème	adv.	this is how…, this way	3
中文	Zhōngwén	n.	Chinese language	1
中午	zhōngwǔ	n.	noon	4
住	zhù	v.	to stay	7
字	zì	n.	character, written word	3

续表

词语 Word/Phrase	拼音 *Pinyin*	词性 Part of Speech	词义 Meaning	课号 Lesson
昨天	zuótiān	n.	yesterday	5
坐	zuò	v.	to take (a means of transportation)	8
做	zuò	v.	to do, to make	3

专有名词 Proper Nouns

词语 Word/Phrase	拼音 *Pinyin*	词义 Meaning	课号 Lesson
		B	
北京	Běijīng	Beijing	7
		D	
大卫	Dàwèi	David	1
点点	Diǎndian	Diandian	2
		M	
墨西哥人	Mòxīgērén	Mexican (person)	1
		N	
尼克	Níkè	Nick	9
		S	
莎莉	Shālì	Sally	1
		W	
王华	Wáng Huá	Wang Hua	1
		Y	
英国人	Yīngguórén	British (person)	1
		Z	
中国	Zhōngguó	China	9
中国人	Zhōngguórén	Chinese (person)	1